Michael Margolis

Viable Democracy

St. Martin's Press   New York

VIABLE DEMOCRACY

Contents

Acknowledgements

I want to acknowledge the help and encouragement I received in writing this book from many friends, colleagues, and students. Special thanks to Jean Blondel, Ian Budge, Michael Lessnoff, Ellen Margolis, Allen Potter, and Bert Rockman for reviewing portions of the manuscript. Additional thanks to Frances Balfour, Donald McFarlan and Neil Middleton of Penguin Books for their editorial advice and their patience. Finally, thanks to two great teachers, Professors J. D. Lewis and Aaron Wildavsky, who started me down these roads when I was their student at Oberlin College.

Introduction : Good Citizen Brown

An Athenian citizen does not neglect the state because
he takes care of his own household; and even those of us
who are engaged in a business have a very fair idea of
politics. We alone regard a man who takes no interest in
public affairs, not as a harmless, but as a useless
character; and if few of us are originators, we are all
sound judges of a policy.
Pericles, *Funeral Oration*, 430 B.C.

I

Good Citizen Brown was born a child of the Enlightenment, but
he was first conceived all the way back at the time of Ancient
Greece. He grew up in the eighteenth and nineteenth centuries,
mostly in Western Europe and North America.

After a youthful flirtation with the mystique of natural rights
he settled down with a maturer utilitarian philosophy of politics.
The off-spring of this settlement have taken the form of varying
arrangements of political institutions, but all have in common
the utilitarian tenet that the primary purpose of government is
to produce the greatest happiness for the greatest number of its
citizens. This can be achieved through rationally planned legislation approved by the citizens or their representatives, designed
to produce more pleasure than pain for the average citizen, if he
obeys rather than disobeys the law.

Citizen Brown is a born optimist. He has faith in the strength
of his own reason and in the ultimate reasonableness of his fellow
citizens. He believes that citizens are fully capable of governing
themselves, and he further believes that the policies he and his
fellow citizens (or their representatives) decide upon will prove to
be better, on the average, than the alternative policies that might

be determined by other groups. Brown holds no truck with those who prefer the wisdom and expertise of kingly rulers or technological planners. For him popular sovereignty is the *sine qua non* of good government.

Brown himself embodies all the traits of a rational well-informed citizen. He makes strenuous efforts to gather information concerning pending government, legislative or administrative action which might affect him. Among other things this entails monitoring the public news media, attending relevant public meetings, and checking information provided by government agencies, interest groups, and political parties. Brown also talks politics with his family, friends, neighbours and workmates, not to mention public officials, when he gets the chance. He writes letters to the editor, and he participates in radio and television phone-ins. At election time Brown is especially active. He reads the party manifestos, studies the candidates' election addresses, and closely watches the course of the campaign. At times he himself has been a candidate, and on these occasions he has been busier than ever presenting his ideas to the electorate. As a responsible citizen, he has of course never failed to cast his vote in any election for which he was an eligible elector.

Up until the time of the Great Depression life was pretty good to Brown. Despite its ups and downs he prospered. In his early days political participation was limited to men of substantial means owning either property or capital or paying some set amount of taxes. The nineteenth century, however, saw growing acceptance of Brown's contention that as the common man prospered, so he would acquire the leisure time and the desire to turn his attention to responsible consideration of the affairs of state. As the century progressed, therefore, various barriers to participation by the common man were removed. Property qualifications were progressively reduced and eventually eliminated; racial and religious qualifications were struck down; hereditary and proprietary political institutions were gradually stripped of their powers while the powers of institutions of the elected representatives of the people were gradually enhanced. By the early twentieth century virtually all artificial barriers to political participation – except that of sex – had been struck down in those countries in which Citizen Brown made his home.

Brown had proved himself both a capable and a flexible political participant. When the first major expansions of the franchise took place, Brown quickly changed his style from that of a country gentleman sending one of his number to a leisurely session of the legislature to that of the hard-working party activist anxious to elect representatives pledged to pursue his party's programme for the benefit of party supporters and the nation. When tensions arising from the drive for rapid assimilation of diverse ethnic, racial, and religious groups into the electorate threatened to break down civil order (and sometimes did so), Brown and others of his ilk worked tirelessly to adjust yet preserve their countries' political institutions. He stood for moderation and tolerance. When the rise of giant industrial firms undercut the *laissez faire* aspects of his early political thought, Brown supported an expanded governmental role in the economy. He accepted ever more complicated legislation, and he even agreed to let new types of regulatory boards and commissions detail and implement such legislation. All this took more of his time, but good citizen that he was, he could offer the polity no less.

By the early 1920s Citizen Brown had begun to feel his age. Even as his latest major triumph, the enfranchisement of women, moved towards completion, he found himself beset by larger and more complicated political problems than he had ever experienced. The great industrial firms, in spite of the measures Brown had supported to control them, continued to expand both horizontally through takeovers of competitive concerns and vertically through absorption of key supply, distribution and marketing networks for the industrial products they manufactured. Moreover, the firms began to mutate. Their stock ownership grew separate from their managerial control, and they began to grow roots and branches in countries other than those in which they were originally incorporated. For Citizen Brown these developments rendered the task of identifying those responsible for the firms' misdeeds more difficult, and they also exacerbated the problem of monitoring the firms' true financial statuses for purposes of determining their net worths, profits, and tax liabilities.

To add to his difficulties Brown was called upon to consider the extent to which the wealth created by the large industrial concerns should be redistributed among the general citizenry; and he was asked also to consider the means by which such redistribution should be effected. The problem assumed some urgency, for growing up beside the industrial firms were an increasing number of trade unions whose primary purpose was to secure a larger share of the wealth for the worker. How should the claims of these members of the proletariat be weighed against the traditional claims of the capitalist classes? The newly founded USSR represented its revolutionary solution for this problem as the only sensible answer. Was this correct, or were there viable alternatives to a socialist revolution? In order to deal effectively with this problem Brown enrolled in a crash course in economics, industrial relations, and the works of Marx and Lenin.

Still Brown got no rest. Rising standards of living meant the average citizen lived longer. This raised a new problem. To what extent should the polity assume the obligation of providing for the growing number of people who lived beyond their years of active contribution to its economy? If the polity was obligated to support its senior citizens, then was it not obligated to support others in need, such as dependent children, the widowed, the sick and disabled? Brown added welfare economics to his list of courses.

The Great Depression forced Brown's hand. He voted to support vast expansions in governmental powers in order to deal with the miseries wrought by the massive economic crisis. The expansions assumed various forms, some radically socialist in nature, some only mildly reformist of the capitalist system; but all had one feature in common – a large complex bureaucracy. And a great bureaucracy, Brown soon learned, is immensely difficult for citizens to control.

By this time our good citizen was becoming exhausted by his responsibilities. Government had grown so tremendously complex that the once routine task of gathering information about pending legislative or administrative action became virtually impossible. Brown had to specialize in a few areas of particular interest to him, and he had to rely upon his elected representative and his fellow citizens to look after others. Imagine his consternation, when his representatives complained that governmental bureaucracies had become so vast that they too could not be sure of what actions were being taken by officers of government in the name of the people! They, like him, began to rely upon specialists among their number to report upon particular areas of interest. And, in some cases, the elected representatives effectively surrendered most of their legislative powers to small committees or to a cabinet.

Good Citizen Brown redoubled his efforts to live up to the high standards of citizenship he had set for himself, but he could not find the time. His boss threatened to sack him if he missed any more days at work in order to attend another of his public meetings, citizen conferences, or educational courses. His wife threatened divorce if he continued to neglect his family responsibilities in order to fulfil his political obligations. His friends wished he would talk about sports, or music or novels or anything but politics, at least once in a while. And this was still the 1930s. The worst was yet to come.

It begun with an assault on his political philosophy. Frustrated and discouraged by the economic disasters of the 1930s, millions who had formerly supported the ideas Brown advocated, abandoned them, turning instead to the simplistic answers offered by fascist political leaders. Fascism promised to remove from citizens the very responsibility for self-government that was the touchstone of Citizen Brown's political philosophy. No longer need the individual citizen be burdened with the problem of policy choice. The fascist leader would make the choices for him in the interest of the state. The individual citizen need only perform his duties and he would prosper. The official doctrines of fascism were discredited following the holocaust of the Second World War, but the notion that the citizen's patriotic duty requires acquiescence to the superior wisdom of his political leaders has come to be used regularly to attack Brown, whenever he criticizes his government's current policies.

After the Second World War came the anomaly of massive peacetime armed forces, often supported by peacetime conscription. Citizen Brown, though he feared a consequent weakening of civilian control of the affairs of state, nonetheless backed this new development, for he saw no other course. The technological advances in weaponry, which resulted from the war, had made it possible for an aggressor to strike a decisive blow in less time than it took to mobilize a civilian population for defence. A constant state of alertness, maintained by a peacetime army, seemed a necessity.

Unfortunately Brown's worst fears were realized. A peacetime army meant yet another government bureaucracy accompanied by all the usual problems of control by citizens of bureaucrats by citizens or their representatives. Modern military bureaucracies presented even severer problems than those to which Brown had grown accustomed. When Citizen Brown or his representatives asked a particularly probing question about the military's policies or practices, they were often told that it could not be fully or frankly answered, for to do so would release secret information. Did they not realize how invaluable secret information could be to a potential enemy? When they called for changes in military policy in response to changes in world politics, however, they sometimes found their arguments discredited by the public release of secret military intelligence arguing the contrary. And when they tried to modify or cut military spending they found themselves opposed by important sections of the population which had become dependent upon peacetime military spending. Although he still tries, Citizen Brown has begun to despair of his ability to control the armed forces. In some countries he has taken to the streets in demonstrations of protest against policies favouring the military.

The need for large standing armies proved to be an unfortunate consequence of post-war technology, but Citizen Brown hoped that its consequences for the lifestyle of the average citizen would prove beneficial. Indeed, the post-war boom in Western countries brought the average citizen unprecedented levels of affluence. Brown had high hopes that the time of plenty was at hand at last. He envisioned a spreading of this affluence not only among the citizens of the richer nations but also to the citizens of poorer nations through export of technological capabilities and through cooperative enterprises fostered by international organizations like the United Nations. And if citizens of poorer nations became more prosperous, was it not likely that they would become more interested in popular participation in government as had their nineteenth-century counterparts in the West?

It did not work out. The citizens of richer nations could barely agree upon minimal changes in the distribution of resources among themselves, let alone make any significant effort to enrich the citizens of poorer nations. Instead of shrinking, the gap between the richer and poorer nations grew larger. And even when their lot improved somewhat, the citizens of poorer nations showed little inclination to adopt Brown's ideas about self-government.

The problems of ecology, however, struck the crushing blow to Brown's vision of prosperous states governed by citizens like himself. It turned out that world energy sources were inadequate to support the world's population at the level of affluence of the Western nations. Furthermore the expansion of population and the depletion of energy sources were threatening to destroy even those standards of living already achieved in the West. If the poorer nations were to achieve significant material progress, resources would have to be redistributed from richer to poorer nations, population growth would have to be curtailed, new types of energy sources would have to be developed, and old types would have to be conserved. The dream of unlimited economic growth based upon unlimited consumption of world energy resources would have to be abandoned, and Good Citizen Brown would have to reconsider the complex problems of maintaining decent standards of living through more efficient use of the resources already at hand.

2

These days Good Citizen Brown feels old and tired. The problems that were straining his capabilities in the 1930s have not disappeared, and the developments of the post-war period have only added to his burden.

Is there any future for Citizen Brown? Should he and his ideas be pensioned off, or can they be revitalized? The question of Brown's future is important because Brown embodies much of the tradition of liberal-democratic thought, the tradition upon which the government institutions in the West were founded. For those of us living in the West his future is our future.

This book concerns the problem of providing viable democratic government in the last decades of the twentieth century. As our story of Good Citizen Brown illustrates, we contend that the citizen of today has lost control of his government. We believe this stems not from the average citizen's personal indolence, indifference, or lack of capacity, but from the inherent impossibility of employing political institutions and processes designed to cope with problems of the eighteenth century to deal with the complex problems of the twentieth. Our ultimate aim, therefore, is to provide an outline of how political institutions and processes can be arranged to cope better with twentieth-century problems, while at the same time preserving the features of popular participation and control, which are central to liberal democracy.

The discussion is presented in three sections. The first section develops and criticizes commonly held views of what constitutes democratic government. The second examines and evaluates so-called realistic theories of democracy – those based upon research into the political behaviour of modern electorates. The final section outlines our own theory of modern democracy. The concern throughout is to work towards a description of democratic government, which takes account of how ordinary citizens can be realistically expected to participate in politics, and which at the same time maintains the fundamental values inherent in more idealistic descriptions of democracy.

Our concern with the problem of modern democracy is by no means uncommon. In the main, however, recent works which have dealt with this subject have fallen into three categories. First, there have been philosophical works re-emphasizing the importance of democratic values for civil society. These works tend to use empirical materials as illustrations, but they rarely attempt to measure how well citizens can fulfil the behavioural assumptions incorporated in their philosophies of politics.[1] The second type have been more or less the mirror images of the first. They are empirically oriented works examining the extent to which the political behaviour of citizens conforms to the requirement of some model of democracy. But the philosophical assumptions behind these models of democracy have remained largely unexamined.[2] The third type have been more interesting. They have compared and contrasted works of the second type with works of the first, and they have been instrumental in pointing out the philosophical shortcomings of empirical models of democracy. Their main problem, from our point of view, is that they nonetheless offer no positive statement about how political institutions and processes can be arranged so that citizens can cope with today's responsibilities of government in a democratic fashion.[3]

We shall develop such a statement. That is our purpose (and our apology) for offering yet another work on modern democracy.

1 · Politics, Democracy, Political Science

... like a dog walking on his hinder legs. It was not done
well, but you were surprised to find it done at all.
Samuel Johnson, 1763.

I

What is Politics? The literature of political science is littered with
formal definitions of politics. Among other things the diligent
reader will find politics defined variously as the exercise of
power;[1] the resolution of group conflict;[2] the authoritative allocation of values and/or resources;[3] or the processes by which
human efforts towards attaining social goals are steered and coordinated.[4] When we are told so much about what politics is, we are
in fact told nothing useful at all.

The purpose of a definition is to help to structure specific
aspects of our environment. When we use a definition we become
like a photographer peering through a camera lens: certain
things, to which we might normally pay little attention, appear
suddenly writ large; others, which we might normally observe,
become hidden from sight. To the extent that any definition
focuses our attention on aspects of the environment which are
relevant to answering questions we may have about how things
work or how people behave in that environment, then it is a good
definition. To the extent that it excludes relevant aspects of the
environment, or to the extent that it muddles those it includes,
then it is a poor definition. Definitions of politics, such as those
mentioned above, which try to specify politics in an *a priori*
fashion, tend to be poor ones.

Take politics as the exercise of power, for instance. Suppose
Harold promises a girl friend Jane that he will give her a big kiss

if she will cast her vote for their mutual acquaintance George. Jane votes for George, and Harold gives her a big kiss. How shall we characterize this bit of politics? Did Harold exercise power over Jane by getting her to vote for George through his promise of a reward? Or did Jane, who intended to vote for George anyhow, pretend to be undecided in order to force Harold to kiss her? Could it be that Jane was really exercising power over Harold? Or was it actually the case that Harold, who knew Jane found him obnoxious, promised to kiss her in the expectation that she would vote against George in order to avoid that promised kiss? In that case Harold tried to exercise his power, but failed. The example is silly, but the point is not. Why try to characterize the relationship between Harold and Jane as the exercise of power? Why not characterize it as a bargaining relationship, an encounter in which each participant has certain resources which he would like to exchange for certain of the other's resources? Defining politics as the exercise of power does not seem to accommodate such bargaining relationships very easily.

Even though defining politics as the exercise of power fails to accommodate certain relationships, such as bargaining among equals, it nonetheless fails to exclude certain other relationships, which we would not ordinarily characterize as politics. As an example, consider two football supporters who get into a row over the merits of their respective teams. Suppose supporter A beats up supporter B in order to stop him from praising team B. Supporter A has certainly exercised his power over supporter B, but we would hardly say the two supporters have just been participating in politics. Defining politics as the exercise of power has not been very helpful in characterizing this situation either. It seems wise, therefore, to abandon this definition.

How about politics as the resolution of group conflict? This definition would exclude our second example, for it could be argued that supporter A and supporter B are not groups, nor are they attempting to resolve their differences. By the same token, fights between bands of supporters would be excluded. There might be some difficulty in accommodating our first example, but it could be argued that Harold and Jane form a specific instance of the bargaining going on between groups of electors who are seeking to resolve their differences through the electoral process. The definition fits various examples of political bargaining between groups far better than does the exercise of power. For instance, Dr Kissinger's role in effecting the disengagement of the Egyptian and Israeli armies following the war of October 1973 clearly emerges as a political one under this definition; it is less clearly political if politics is defined only as Dr Kissinger's ability to force the contending parties to agree through the threat of a sanction or the promise of a reward from his government, the United States.

But defining politics as the resolution of group conflict has its problems. Numerous studies have shown that even in highly organized countries like Great Britain or the United States over one third of the adult population claim no group memberships whatsoever.[5] Some twenty per cent or more rarely even vote. Are we to say that by definition these citizens do not participate in politics? And what about those primitive societies in which anthropologists report there are no recognizable organizational structures? Are we to say that by definition these societies have no politics? Defining politics as the resolution of group conflict seems to leave out too much. Perhaps it too should be abandoned.

Yet the other two definitions listed – the authoritative allocation of values and the coordination of effort to achieve social goals – are similarly open to objections. Does it really help our analysis of the rationship between Harold and Jane if we think of it as political only because George, once elected, will have authority to allocate social values or to coordinate citizens' efforts to achieve goals? It seems not. And what if the election is only for officers of a social club, the membership of which is entirely voluntary? Are we still talking about politics, or must politics be limited to agencies with some authority or with responsibility for solving problems or achieving goals of a public nature?

What we are driving at boils down to this: it is perfectly

possible to employ any of the above discussed definitions of politics, or indeed to employ other definitions *a priori*, but there is little to gain from doing so. Notwithstanding the intellectual devotion that has been lavished on this or that definition, there has never been to our knowledge a convincing demonstration that any *a priori* definition of politics surpasses all others in terms of its usefulness for structuring our observations about human behaviour. Every *a priori* definition of politics that we have ever come across has been open to the sorts of objections which were raised to each of the definitions discussed above. To paraphrase Dr Johnson, after all these years of trying to define politics *a priori*, we are no longer surprised that it is not done well – we are surprised to find it done at all!

Politics is whatever we make it. In our roles as citizens, politicians, journalists, commentators or researchers we define politics *a posteriori*. In each case it is incumbent upon us to demonstrate the usefulness of applying the label politics to the behaviours and events we have designated as politics. There seems to be no realm of human endeavour that we may dismiss out of hand as never involving politics.

To return to our first example, it would be useful to treat the interchange between Harold and Jane as a relevant instance of politics, if we were concerned with how political participants employ their resources to seek their desired ends or how voters make up their minds in an election. But if our concerns were focused on how public policies are made, and this particular election were for officers of a social club, then it would no longer be very useful to designate Harold and Jane's relationship as an instance of politics.

To recapitulate our main points: (1) the criterion for determining a good definition is its usefulness for structuring our observations of evidence relevant to the questions we are asking; (2) *a priori* definitions of politics do not satisfy this criterion; (3) therefore, we suggest abandoning them in favour of defining politics *a posteriori*, in the immediate context with which we are concerned.

2

Political Participation and Democracy. As we argued that politics is more usefully left to *a posteriori* specification than to *a priori* definition, so we contend that participation in politics is also more usefully determined after, rather than before, empirical observation.

What is considered to be participation varies greatly not only among different societies and cultures but also within the same societies and cultures over time. The works of Theodore Roosevelt and Jacobus Ten Broek, which describe respectively the incompetence of US army supply and transport during the Spanish-American war and the deportation of Japanese-Americans to concentration camps during the Second World War, are generally considered to be works of historical and scholarly interest.[6] As the recent exile of Alexander Sohlzenitsyn demonstrated, however, his works, which describe the incompetence of the Russian Army at the start of the First World War and the deportations of citizens to forced labour camps during the Stalinist era, are considered to be political tracts which slander the government of the USSR.[7] Until recently an American woman who publicly announced she had had an abortion for reasons other than her immediate physical well-being was committing a political act designed to test the constitutionality of the anti-abortion laws of her home state. If abortion becomes accepted practice, it is conceivable that sometime in the future an American woman with two children who announces she will *not* have her subsequent pregnancies aborted will be committing a political act.

How can we construct a useful definition of political participation *a priori* in order to cover circumstances as diverse as these? We see no advantage to be gained from the attempt. Political participation, like politics itself, is best left to *a posteriori* specification.

This sort of argument should not be pushed too far, however. Even though we find great diversity among polities calling themselves democracies, we shall not be so obstreperous as to argue that democracy should not be defined. Instead we shall build upon our previously undefined terms in order to construct *a priori* definitions of democratic politics and of democracy. We define democratic politics as that form of politics in which each citizen in the polity has an equal opportunity to participate. A democracy, then, is a polity in which democratic politics is the only politics.

Our definitions manifestly illustrate the advantages of leaving politics and political participation undefined *a priori*. Because these terms are undefined, our definitions of democratic politics and of democracy become universal ones, applicable to any polity once its politics and modes of participation in its politics are specified. In principle, scales could be developed to measure the extent to which citizens have equal opportunities to participate. Such scales would allow us to compare the extent to which any two polities were democratic.

In practice the job is not so easy. Complete specification of the politics and modes of political participation of a given polity is a burdensome if not impossible task. Nonetheless it is possible to specify particular aspects or areas of politics about which we wish to inquire. We can then measure the extent to which we in fact find equal opportunity for citizens to participate in these aspects or areas. By comparing these measurements with measurements taken for equivalent aspects or areas of politics of other polities, we can indeeed decide upon the relative extent to which democratic politics is found in specified areas of politics of any two polities.

This is not as complicated as it sounds. What we are saying is that we may look at selected aspects of politics instead of trying to specify everything. Thus we can make comparisons between such features as manners of electing representatives, or procedures for arriving at administrative policy decisions in two different polities, and we may comment on the extent to which these aspects of politics are democratic. Furthermore, if we find certain equivalencies, for example that formal membership in a political party in polity A is equivalent to formal membership in a trade union in polity B, we may compare the opportunities for political participation for members of political parties in polity A with the opportunities for political participation for the members of trade unions in polity B in order to determine the extent to which these equivalent aspects of politics are democratic in these polities.[8]

The concept of equal opportunity is fundamental to our definition of democracy. However, there is disagreement among democratic theorists over how equal opportunity should be measured. No democratic theorist argues in favour of unequal opportunity, but many are quick to accuse those who disagree with them of holding such a position. In our subsequent discussion we shall pay particular attention to two major questions involved in this controversy; namely; to what extent do (1) systems of elective representation or (2) inequalities in the distribution of economic resources necessarily destroy equal opportunities for participation in politics?

In spite of complications about how equal opportunity should be measured, we believe that our *a priori* definitions will prove useful. To begin with they do not limit our attention to some particular number of nation-states. In fact the polities referred to in the definitions need not be nation-states at all – they can be any recognizable collectivity from the family to the international community. So we expect to talk about the politics of collectivities other than the nation-state, and we expect it will be useful to examine the extent to which such politics can be characterized as democratic.

In addition our definitions of democratic politics and democracy do not carry along the excess baggage of specific political institutions. We stipulate no institutional requirements like those of a prime minister and parliament or a president and congress. Nor is there any mention of periodic elections, fundamental laws, or independent judiciaries. The emphasis is placed upon the empirically measurable characteristic of equal opportunity for political participation. We believe the question of whether or not the political institutions of a given polity facilitate such opportunity can be answered best through empirical investigation.

Nor do our definitions make mention of any specific policy outcomes or collective goals. We look at democratic politics as a process, one which may produce results which we as observers do not approve. We expect that citizens of a democracy will attempt to preserve that democracy by avoiding policy outcomes which impair the opportunity for further participation in politics of some of their fellow citizens, but this expectation must be tested in each case by empirical observation.

Finally, we do not include majority rule in our definitions. Why? Because there seems little reason to object to a situation where a minority makes decisions for the polity, provided that each member of the collectivity has equal opportunity to participate in the politics of selecting the decision-making minority. Why should a majority be required to participate in all collective decisions? If the majority feel that the time and effort involved in participating in politics amounts to more than the time and effort required to satisfy the obligations created by the decision-making minority, or to rectify its misdeeds, why should they bother to participate? Readers need only think of any organization – a social club, a church group, an athletic team, a trade union or professional organization – with which they are familiar. The chances are that important decisions for the organization are taken by a designated minority, most likely an elected set of officers or a committee appointed by those officers. Despite this obvious condition of minority rule, many readers will nonetheless consider their organizations to be democratic. We submit that the crucial consideration here is opportunity for political participation, not majority rule.

3

Political Science. We define political science as the systematic study of how people participate in politics. We believe this is a useful definition, for it specifies particular aims; yet it is not limited to particular cultures or collectivities.

The definition makes clear that political science is concerned with the behaviour of people, not ants, stars, or molecules. Furthermore, it stipulates an empirical mode of investigation. Political science does not deal with *a priori* justifications of values nor with proofs of abstract propositions, such as those of formal mathematics. Finally, political science is systematic. Political scientists employ their concepts and observations of political behaviour to build upon their previous knowledge. Their constant aim is the detection, explanation and prediction of patterns of participation in politics.

In subsequent chapters we shall often refer to the findings of political science, and we shall use them to confront the empirical assumptions contained in the theories of democracy we shall examine. We shall also take explicit account of them when we propose our own theory of democracy in chapter 7.

2 · Liberal Democracy

We hold these truths to be self-evident, that all men are
created equal, that they are endowed by their Creator
with certain inalienable Rights, that among these are
Life, Liberty, and the pursuit of Happiness – That to
secure these Rights, Governments are instituted among
Men, deriving their just powers from the consent of the
governed – That whenever any Form of Government
becomes destructive of these ends, it is the Right of the
People to alter or abolish it, and to institute a new
Government ...
Thomas Jefferson, 'Declaration of Independence', 1776.

Ask not what your country can do for you – ask what
you can do for your country.
John F. Kennedy, 'Inaugural Address', 1961

I

Liberalism and Democracy. The tenets of liberal democracy lie
at the core of Anglo-American political institutions. Basically
liberal democracy emphasizes facilitation of individual self-
development and self-expression as the primary goals of government. The object of government is to keep open for the individual a wide range of options and values. There should be no
premature closure of alternatives and, in so far as possible, any
set of chosen alternatives should not be viewed as permanent.

Liberal democracy views men as rational beings, capable of
examining alternatives and deciding upon those which serve their
own best interests. To this end, liberal democracy emphasizes
citizen participation in politics as a means of achieving personally desired goals.

Liberal democracy is also optimistic about men's behaviour. It

26

assumes that rational participation in politics will serve to develop not only the individual's own interests but will also impart to him an appreciation of broader considerations such as those of his fellow citizens or of the society as a whole. Furthermore, liberal democracy believes that for any given society there exist discoverable sets of mutually compatible values and goals among the general citizenry, which form a common interest or general will. Although these values and goals vary by time and by place, the fundamental premise is that the interests of men are basically harmonious.

Liberal democracy, however, is not synonymous with democracy itself; it is a rather special type of democracy. Governments can be democratic without being liberal. Conversely they can be liberal without being democratic.[1]

The USSR, for example, lays claim to being a democracy, though it certainly is not a liberal one. Certain goals and values, such as those of private capitalism, Judaism, Trotskyism, and other forms of revisionism, are ruled out as questions of choice. Others, such as those of Marxist-Leninist communism, atheism, and peaceful competition with capitalist countries are accepted as incontrovertible truth. Within the framework of these accepted goals and values, however, a vigorous democratic politics may be pursued. Each citizen has ample opportunity to express his opinions, vote, seek office – in short, to participate, however he chooses – the only condition being that he stick within that framework of accepted goals and values.

The governments of Britain and the United States, on the other hand, provide us with examples of liberalism without democracy. Throughout the nineteenth and early twentieth centuries, the basically liberal goals of these governments never varied. Individual self-development was a primary goal. So much so that many prominent politicians and political writers even advocated complete *laissez-faire* policies for government not only with regard to traditional political rights such as freedoms of speech, assembly, worship, and of the press, but also with regard to economic matters, such as wages and conditions of employment, marketing operations of monopolistic enterprises, and negotiation of all forms of contracts. Nevertheless over this same

27

period of time large groups of Britons and Americans were denied equal opportunity for political participation because of race, sex, or economic status. Slavery was maintained in the United States until 1865. The bulk of the working class was disenfranchised in Britain until 1884. And in both countries women had to wait until the third decade of the twentieth century to achieve equal opportunity to vote.

Liberalism itself can be further divided into two forms. The first form shares the optimistic faith of liberal democracy that individual interests of citizens are fundamentally compatible. The second has no such faith. It stresses the need for a stable structure of rules to govern men's conduct – a system of law and order. Otherwise men might selfishly pursue incompatible ends, which would ultimately result in a breakdown of society and a consequent loss of all opportunity for individual self-development. The first form leads to revolutionary sorts of political philosophies emphasizing the subordination of interests of the state to those of the individual. The second leads to more conservative philosophies emphasizing the necessity of a well-ordered state before individual interests can be served.

2

Social Contract. Social contract is a basically liberal notion. It assumes men are rational beings, desirous of improving themselves. To this end they 'contract in' to form societies, the purpose of which is to facilitate their members' self-fulfilment. In its revolutionary form social contract emphasizes the rights of citizens and provides the original liberal-democratic justification for the establishment of the popularly chosen institutions of government of modern Britain and the United States. In its conservative form social contract emphasizes the importance of community interests and the virtues of orderliness, moderation and gradualism so often cited by political leaders today.

The establishment of the rights of the people and the powers of popularly chosen institutions of government in their modern form in Britain and the United States dates from the Glorious Revolution of 1688 and the American Revolution of 1776. The ideas of social contract used to justify these revolutions were developed by the English philosopher, John Locke (1632–1704), and modified by the American statesman, Thomas Jefferson (1743–1826).

In his *Second Treatise on Civil Government* (first published in 1690) Locke developed a political theory which, though intended primarily as apology for the Glorious Revolution, had far broader implications. Locke began with the premise that men are basically reasonable. It followed that most men could live together harmoniously in an unorganized society – a hypothetical state of nature – in accordance with the dictates of the laws of nature. Such laws were discoverable through proper application of reason and observation. Men find it prudent to form societies or commonwealths, however, to secure their natural rights and liberties against those few unreasonable individuals who lack a proper understanding of natural law. Societies are formed by mutual consent: each person agrees to give up his individual power to punish transgressions of the laws of nature and to act as he sees fit for the preservation of himself and others; in return, it becomes the duty of the community to punish such transgressions and to preserve each citizen's natural rights. Locke called this agreement the contract of commonwealth.

Once incorporated, the commonwealth may choose to set up whatever form of government it desires. Citizens agree by mutual consent to entrust specified powers to particular individuals who then carry out the functions of government. The conditions of the trust are that the governing officials carry out their functions in such a manner as to protect the natural rights – the life, liberty, and property – of the individual citizens. This latter agreement is often called the contract of government.

Should the citizens judge that the governmental officials have violated the conditions of trust, they may dissolve the government, reclaim the power, and institute a new government. The importance of the two contracts should be apparent: citizens may dissolve the government (cancel the second contract) without destroying the society or commonwealth (without cancelling the first contract).

Essentially all Jefferson did was apply Locke's principles to the contemporary American situation. Jefferson argued that the currently reigning King, George III, had repeatedly violated the colonists' rights as subjects of the Crown. Disdaining the colonists' petitions for redress of grievances (a right explicitly guaranteed by the Declaration of Rights of 1689), the King seemed bent upon establishing an 'absolute Tyranny' over the colonies. Such disgraceful behaviour vitiated the reasons for which government had been instituted. The American colonists were left with no choice: 'it is their right, it is their duty, to throw off such a Government, and to provide new Guards for their future Security.'[2]

Although his fundamental principles were derived from Locke's, Jefferson was bolder than his intellectual master. His justification of revolution preceded rather than followed the actual overthrow of the government, and his view of natural rights was broader and less tied to property. He opposed even constitutional monarchy, and he thought that a revolution in the cause of liberty every decade or two was the sign of a healthy society.[3]

Locke and Jefferson both stressed that the individual citizen's rights are prior to and more important than any obligations he owes to the state. Government is the servant of the people. The officers of government hold their positions at the sufferance of the people. Their job is to ensure that the rights of the people are preserved and protected by government. Citizens come first; government comes second.

We are familiar with these revolutionary ideas, for as mentioned above, they form the liberal-democratic justification for the political institutions which have become a part of the Anglo-American heritage. These ideas are preached from the pulpit; they are taught in the schools. We have become so familiar with them that we recite them, as we sometimes recite the Lord's Prayer – without thinking about what we actually say. Or worse yet, we stop thinking about their meaning altogether, and we come to accept conservative ideas of social contract as if they were the same thing.

A perfect example of this is the widespread acceptance of the conservative sentiments contained in the famous quotation from John F. Kennedy's 'Inaugural Address' inserted at the beginning of this chapter. Juxtaposed against Jefferson's argument in the 'Declaration of Independence', the fact that Kennedy had inverted the traditional relationship of citizen to government – placed the interests of the latter before those of the former, becomes starkly apparent. But Kennedy was known as a liberal democrat, and so his statement was quoted as if it were in accord with the mainstream of liberal-democratic ideas.

In fact Kennedy's statement accords with the conservative school of social contract – at least if it is interpreted to imply that a citizen must serve his country in order to produce benefits which each citizen can individually enjoy. As mentioned, this form of social contract stresses the importance of law and order. Its seventeenth-century spokesman was Thomas Hobbes (1588–1679).

Hobbes's most famous work, *Leviathan*, published in 1651, was written in reaction to the disorders caused by the English civil wars, which had culminated with the execution of King Charles I. Hobbes perceived men as rational beings, but unlike Locke and Jefferson, he had no faith in their abilities to live in harmony with one another without a government. The trouble was, as Hobbes saw it, that men were basically selfish, that the strong would take from the weak. But the weak, being rational, would in turn band together against the strong. For Hobbes the state of nature became a chaotic state in which every man becomes the enemy of every other. It became a war of all against all – with ghastly consequences for everyone:

> In such condition there is no place for industry, because the fruit thereupon is uncertain, and consequently no culture of the earth; no navigation nor use of the commodities that may be imported by sea; no commodious building; no instruments of moving or removing such things as require much force; no knowledge of the face of the earth; no account of time, no arts; no letters; no society; and, which is worst of all, continual fear and danger of violent death; and the life of man solitary, poor, nasty, brutish, and short.[4]

The solution proposed by Hobbes was for the citizens to enter into a contract of commonwealth with one another. This contract resembled Locke's only in name. The conditions of the contract were that each citizen agree to surrender all his powers to a sovereign power, the Leviathan, on condition that every other citizen do the same. The Leviathan would protect the citizens of the commonwealth and would provide a system of law and order. In return the citizens owed the Leviathan their absolute obedience. There was only one contract. To break it would return men back to the chaotic state of nature. The only reason for disobeying the Leviathan, therefore, was if he failed in his first duty – that of protecting the life and limb of the citizens.

The important point here is that Hobbes's aims were basically liberal. He wanted to produce a society in which men would be free to enjoy the fruits of their labours. His lack of faith in their ability to govern themselves forced him to conclude that an absolute ruler was necessary in order to bring about the desired liberal society.

Kennedy, of course, was not the only modern statesman to make an argument which seems more compatible with the ideas of Hobbes than with those of Locke and Jefferson. How often have we been bombarded recently with arguments urging the need for greater amounts of law and order – stricter enforcement of existing laws, passage of more severe regulations, a return to birching or even hanging – even at the expense of the rights of some individuals, particularly the accused? And why is there such a need? Because modern civilization will break down unless drastic steps are taken comes the answer. Study the latest statistics on crimes of violence we are told. How can the relentless increase of such crimes be curtailed, if not by increased doses of law and order? In a similar vein political leaders tell us that individual rights of dissent must be suppressed, in order to bring about the national unity required to defend ourselves against the external enemies who will otherwise destroy our civilization. National security is a concept Hobbes would have understood.

Kennedy's statement is also compatible with the less absolutist, though still conservative, statement of social contract (*Du Contrat Social*), published by Jean-Jacques Rousseau in 1762. Unlike Hobbes, Rousseau (1712–78) did not view the state of nature as one of absolute chaos. The problem as Rousseau saw it was that the natural harmony of the state of nature was due to men's intuitive goodness not to their reason. The latter only

32

developed in civil society. The intuitive goodness was easily overwhelmed by conventional arguments for social institutions, which likened rulers to father figures, and extolled the virtues of obedience to such figures. To a remarkable extent strong leaders have in Rousseau's judgement already succeeded not only in extracting obedience from citizens, but also in justifying such obedience.

'Man is born free, and everywhere he is in chains,' he observed.[5] And later:

> The strongest is never strong enough to be always the master, unless he transforms his might into right, and obedience into duty. Hence the right of the strongest, a 'right' which looks like an ironical pleasantry, but in fact is a well-established principle.[6]

But Rousseau denied that might made right. The only authority which citizens ought to obey is a legitimate one. And the only legitimate authority would be one which:

> defends and protects the person and property of each member with the whole force of the community, and where each, while joining with all the rest, still obeys no one but himself ...[7]

The solution is the social contract, a contract which bears a strong resemblance in form to that of Hobbes. The terms are that each individual alienates all his rights, not just certain rights, to the community as a whole. But this community as a whole is not an independent force like Hobbes's *Leviathan*. Rather it is an expression of the general will of the citizens themselves. By means of it each citizen becomes the author and the subject of every governmental act. He exchanges the primative freedom of the state of nature for the higher freedom to follow the general will.

If Rousseau's social contract seems less clearly formulated than those of Locke or Hobbes, it need not worry us greatly. The coherence of Rousseau's argument is as much psychological as logical. The sovereign power he tried to create was one which could not harm the individual members of the community because it was composed of them. What Rousseau sought was to unite the individual citizen with the sovereign in such a strong psychological bond that the citizen would submit to the general will even though his private interest might seem to the contrary. At the same time Rousseau wanted the submission of private interests to the general will to involve no real sacrifice, for the general will represented what the citizen really wanted as a citizen of a community as opposed to what he might want as a selfish individual. Indeed if the whole of the community forced a dissenter to conform to the general will, it never bothered Rousseau, for such coercion 'means nothing more or less than that he will be forced to be free'.[8] For Rousseau conformity to the general will was the highest form of freedom. Obeying the general will was nothing more than obeying what one would will as best for oneself.

Rousseau's most direct influence was upon the French Revolution. The French 'Declaration of the Rights of Man and the Citizen' (1789) explicitly recognized the sovereignty of the general will expressed in law. And in contrast to the American 'Declaration of Independence' it contains explicit mention of obligations and duties of the citizen, such as assenting to taxes in support of military or police forces for the community. In modern times Rousseauian influence can be found in various constitutions and charters of communities which make note of similar obligations or duties of citizens, or in laws, such as those of Belgium or Australia, which make the obligation to vote compulsory.

3

Utilitarianism. Notwithstanding their different views of the importance of community interests relative to the interests of the individual citizen, the social-contract theories we have discussed all share one important characteristic: they assume that men have natural rights, which they wish to preserve and protect through the social contract. Locke and Jefferson are most specific in listing such rights, but even Hobbes and Rousseau mention rights to defend one's life and to acquire property.

The self-evident nature of men's rights was destroyed utterly by the reasoning of David Hume (1711–76). In two important works, *A Treatise of Human Nature* (1739) and an *Inquiry Concerning Human Understanding* (1749), Hume distinguished between the logical standing of proofs of mathematics and the logical standing of causal relations between matters of fact. The former contain logically necessary statements, but they tell us nothing about matters of fact. The latter contain no logically necessary statements; they merely state empirical correlations.

To illustrate Hume's points, let us consider the following argument: (1) No American President is a crook; (2) Richard M. Nixon is an American President; (3) Mr Nixon, therefore, is not a crook. This argument, although logically correct, neither proves nor disproves that Mr Nixon is not a crook. It says no more about the real world than does its totally abstract form: (1) No A is a B; (2) N is an A; (3) N, therefore, is not a B. Indeed, whether or not Mr Nixon is a crook is a question of fact, and like all questions of fact, it can be ascertained only by empirical investigation. It is not subject to logical deduction by reason alone, nor for that matter can the answer be provided to us by personal intuition or even by divine revelation.

Empirical truths are discovered from empirical investigation. Causal relationships are induced from empirically observed regularities. The truth of such relationships, however, does not have the same eternal verity as the truths of logical analysis. For example, take the following proposition: Labour governments cause more inflation than their Conservative predecessors. Let us suppose that a thorough investigation of all Labour governments reveals that the proposition is true. There is always the chance that the next Labour government will pursue economic policies which produce less inflation than did their predecessor's policies and that the proposition will therefore be invalidated.

Hume was enough of a sceptic to point out that even the laws of the physical sciences were based upon empirical correlation rather than logical deduction. There is no logical reason why the sun should rise again tomorrow, or why the next ripe apple should fall to the earth and not to the sky. There is merely the fact that these events have always been observed to occur in the expected manner. Of course we accept physical laws as real truths, and we act upon them. We even risk our lives on them, for example, whenever we decide to fly in an aeroplane or to rely upon the brakes of a car.

If physical laws had such shaky logical foundations, then how much more unstable were the foundations of the so-called natural laws or natural rights, which social-contract theorists claimed to have discovered? There was, Hume demonstrated, neither a logical nor an empirical proof of their truth. All men were created equal, not by natural law, but by social convention to treat them equal. Men had natural rights to life, liberty and property, only if social conventions allowed them. The democratic ends described by social-contract theorists had to be accepted on faith; there were no logically valid arguments to support them.

If governments were not formed to preserve natural rights, then what purposes did they serve? Hume answered that governments were conventional structures which served the common interest by implementing general rules or values which had been shown by experience to serve human needs. Governments were based upon the utility of these rules not their eternal truth.

Not everyone of Hume's contemporaries was prepared to accept his arguments. Jefferson was aware of them, and he explicitly rejected them. Rousseau attempted to incorporate them into his arguments, referring to the social contract as a social convention designed to legitimate the sovereign power, but he never quite gave up the idea of men's natural rights to life and property. (Locke and Hobbes had died before Hume was born.) By the nineteenth century, however, Hume's separation of logical necessity from empirical correlation had come to be the dominant philosophical position, and justifications of government moved away from social contract and towards utilitarianism.

Utilitarianism amounts to little more than eighteenth-century liberalism in new clothing. The values of individual self-development and self-aggrandizement remain paramount. So, too, remains the liberal desire for a variety of choices, the repugnance for regimentation. Only the justification is different. The basis of government is utility, not contract. People are motivated by feelings of pleasure and pain. They will obey the law so long as the inconveniences of obedience are outweighed by the pains of disobedience. The morality of mankind can be regulated, therefore, by judicious design and application of the law. The principle behind all law should be to produce the greatest happiness (most pleasure and least pain) for the greatest number of citizens. Liberal government is useful to rational citizens because of the pleasures they derive from the freedoms it provides. Real rights are provided by real laws; there is no need for the myths of natural rights or social contract.

The greatest exponent of the utilitarian position was Jeremy Bentham (1748–1832). In two important works, the *Fragment on Government* (1776) and the *Principles of Morals and Legislation* (1789), he developed the basic utilitarian arguments described in the previous paragraph. Indeed he pushed these arguments even further. He argued that the interests of the community amounted to the sum of the interests of the citizens who compose it, and he tried to supply a calculus for determining the amounts of pleasure and pain the individual derived from any political act.

The immediate upshot of Bentham's works was the implementation of widespread reform of British penal law. The famous notion that properly fitted penalties ought to deter crime is a direct consequence of Bentham's reasoning. The longer term consequence of Bentham's works was the electoral reforms beginning in 1832. If government's mission is to provide the greatest happiness for the greatest number, and if each citizen's interest counts equally in determining the common interest, then it follows that each citizen ought to have equal opportunity to express his interest to government so that government can take it into acount when formulating policies to promote the general happiness of all citizens. From 1808 until his death in 1832, Bentham himself turned his attentions from advocacy of legal and penal reform to advocacy of electoral reform as well.[9]

It was through the influence of James Mill (1773–1836), whom he met in 1808, that Bentham became convinced that his own ideas inevitably led to electoral as well as legal and penal reform. Bentham had become frustrated by government indifference to his plans for a model prison with facilities geared towards reforming rather than punishing its clientele. Mill provided him with an explanation of why he had been frustrated.

If, as Bentham said, men were motivated by feelings of pleasure and pain, was it not likely that a few selfish individuals might seek the power necessary to render their fellows subservient to their particular whims and fancies? Indeed, according to Mill, British government as it then stood was far too 'aristocratical'. The overly restrictive franchise had left too few individuals in control. They could run government primarily for the benefit of themselves and their small bands of supporters without ever having to worry about retribution for their abuses at the polls. The general public lacked the power to displace them. The solution, Mill suggested, was to broaden the franchise in order to achieve a proper balance between aristocratical (and monarchical) elements on the one hand and democratical elements on the other. The broadened franchise should be accompanied by reasonably short parliaments. With these reforms representatives would be likely to forgo or at least temper their abuses, for there existed a real threat of their imminent demotion to the status of *hoi polloi* at the next election. What rational representative would be so foolish as to legislate burdens for the ordinary citizen which were too onerous for he himself to assume, should he lose his privileged status? Mill reasoned that through proper institutional arrangements men's selfishness could be channelled towards public policies which generated the greatest good for the greatest number.

Mill did much to popularize the way Bentham's ideas applied to government in Britain, particularly through his *Essay on Government* which appeared as a supplement to the 1820 edition of the *Encyclopaedia Britannica* and later in book form. It remained for his son, John Stuart Mill (1806–1873), to refine and alter Bentham's thought.

The impetus of Bentham and the elder Mill's political thought had been to democratize British political institutions. In America this democratization had proceeded at a faster pace, and by the 1830s the suffrage had been granted to nearly all adult white males. American democracy had produced a robust electoral politics engaged in by a brash self-confident citizenry. Insofar as these consequences conformed to the expectations of liberal-democratic thought, they were welcomed. But a new danger arose from them – a subtle tyranny of the majority. As described by the Frenchman, Alexis de Tocqueville (1805–1859), in *Democracy in America* (1835), citizens of many American communities were so agreed upon political opinions and popular morality that the majority often felt free to force the relatively few dissenters to conform to the dominant position or else to suffer social ostracism or other forms of social or economic pressure. In short democracy without liberalism was an emerging pattern of American politics.

In his great essay, *On Liberty*, published in 1859, the younger Mill took up de Tocqueville's points, for by this time they applied to Britain as well as to America. As Mill saw it government was rapidly becoming the province of the average man and, unless institutional arrangements were made to discourage it, enforced conformity to the opinions and morality of the average man would become the lot of all citizens.

Echoing Hume's point about the uncertainty of claims of absolute truth, particularly about abstract questions of morality or natural law, Mill argued that stifling a minority opinion was in effect making an unjustified claim of infallibility for the dominant opinion. The best approximation to the truth normally would be reached through the freest possible interchange of opinions and ideas, however conflicting. There was virtually no justifiable reason for interfering with liberty of possession, and the only proper reason for interfering with anyone's liberty of action was self protection. Interfering with someone's liberty for 'his own good' was not sufficient warrant. In practice such interference led to ridiculous regulations like temperance laws or sabbath restrictions. 'The only freedom which deserves the name', he stated, 'is that of pursuing our own good in our own way, so long as we do not attempt to deprive others of theirs, or impede their efforts to obtain it.'[10]

But this argument is hardly utilitarian. If men are motivated by pleasure and pain, and if a given amount of pleasure for one man counts no more than the same amount of pleasure for another, then does not conformity to the opinions of majority produce the greatest pleasure for the greatest number? Could Mill's argument be justified on utilitarian grounds?

In *Utilitarianism* (1861) Mill took up this point. Quite simply he argued that there were different refinements of pleasure. Human beings rarely longed to become beasts even though they might escape the stress of human affairs and gain all the animal pleasures of (for instance) the contented cow. The pleasures enjoyed by human beings were of a far better quality; they were well worth the pains then sometimes experienced. Furthermore, among the pleasures humans enjoyed, there were different qualities. The pleasure derived from reading a good book normally ought to count for more than the pleasure derived from having a pint at the local pub. In general the pleasures of the intellect should count for more than the pleasures of the flesh. Of course Mill had no way of proving these last two assertions. Instead he appealed to the mass of experienced opinion:

> On a question which is the best worth having of two pleasures, or which of two modes of existence is the most grateful to the feelings, apart from its moral attributes and from its consequences, the judgement of those who are qualified by knowledge of both, or, if they differ, that of the majority among them, must be admitted as final.[11]

Based upon his own experience, Mill did expect that qualified judges would tend to rate intellectual pleasures highest. In fact Mill confidently expected that with increased educational opportunities for the masses the quality of pleasure would increase, for the average citizen would come to understand that his own happiness was inexorably bound up in the happiness of the entire community and would act accordingly, taking the interests of others into account.

In *Considerations on Representative Government* (1861) he discussed the environmental factors necessary to bring about the type of liberal-democratic state he had in mind. Mill suggested that neither democratic institutions of government nor traditions of democratic rule provided adequate safeguards for liberty. The crucial factor was the quality of the electorate, their collective commitment to individual freedom in particular:

> But there are also cases in which, though not averse to a form of government – possibly even desiring it – a people may be unwilling or unable to fulfil its conditions. They may be incapable of fulfilling such of them as are necessary to keep the government even in normal existence. Thus, a people may prefer a free government, but if, from indolence, or carelessness, or cowardice, or want of public spirit, they

are unequal to the exertions necessary for preserving it; if they will not fight for it when it is directly attacked; if they can be deluded by the artifices used to cheat them out of it; if by momentary discouragement, or temporary panic, or a fit of enthusiasm for an individual, they can be induced to lay their liberties at the feet even of a great man, or trust him with powers which enable him to subvert their institutions; in all these cases they are more or less unfit for liberty; and though it may be for their good to have had it, even for a short time, they are unlikely long to enjoy it.[12]

In spite of his reservations about tyranny of the majority Mill was quite an advanced democrat for his time. He favoured universal suffrage for the educated electorate with no discrimination against a citizen for reasons of race, sex, religion, or other arbitrary factors. He encouraged political participation, because he believed that democratic politics itself was an educative process. The citizen who followed public affairs, voted, and otherwise took his responsibilities seriously, would in addition to protecting his own interests gain a broader knowledge and greater appreciation of the needs of the community as a whole. The citizen would thereby have become more educated, and could apply his knowledge for his own and the community's benefit.

4

Liberal Democracy Today. The ideas of social contract and utilitarianism still furnish the foundations for liberal-democratic thought. Good Citizen Brown, whom we met in the Introduction, seemed so familiar because his basic attitudes reflected these ideas. The changes in liberal-democratic thought, which have taken place since John Stuart Mill's time, are really just dross. Despite their twentieth-century labels – democratic socialism, welfare statism, social and economic planning – the fundamental aims of liberal-democratic governments remain the facilitation of individual self-expression, self-development and self-aggrandizement.

Even the institutional structures have remained the same. We find an executive branch of government, a legislative, and a judicial. The head of executive branch is normally elected either directly by the people, or indirectly by their representatives. The legislative is normally divided into two houses, at least one of which is directly elected for relatively short terms of office. The legislative branch officially controls the public purse. The judicial branch is either appointed by the other branches or elected by the people for relatively long terms of office, often for life. Once in office, members of the judicial branch normally are protected from intimidation by the other two branches of government or by the people themselves.

The institutional structure is designed to accomplish James Mill's aim of balanced government. The separate branches of government are expected to draw support from different groups or classes of citizens. The representatives of these various classes will work to enhance the powers of the institutions of government they control. With proper constitutional arrangements, the separate branches will check one another, and the officers of those branches will be forced to bargain and compromise with one another in order for government to function. In short to achieve any of their selfish aims, representatives of one class will have to consider the aims and interests of those of other classes.[13]

Whether such institutional arrangements still work is a moot point. The growth of modern bureaucracy already noted in our introduction may well have rendered the legislative and judicial branches subordinate to the executive. And whether such arrangements are adequate for dealing with problems which were insignificant or indeed unheard of a century ago is also moot. How is a national government supposed to deal with an international corporation or an international problem like the energy shortage or environmental pollution? How can the people's representatives deal with complex technological problems ranging from health and welfare planning to military preparedness? How can the citizenry make their opinions and preferences about the vast array of problems governments are concerned with known to their representatives?

But the critique of liberal democracy is not limited to the questioning of the adequacy of governmental structures which have been used to implement it. There are more fundamental critiques which question the assumptions it makes concerning

the rationality of men, the feasibility of representative government and the economic order of the society in which representative government operates. It is to these types of critiques we first
turn our attention, for their roots lie in the eighteenth and nineteenth centuries, the same period from which the mainstream of
liberal-democratic thought emerged.

3 · Critiques of Liberal Democracy

Types of Critiques. The values of liberal democracy, whether justified by social contract or social utility, nonetheless placed the welfare of the individual citizen over and above that of the community. Even when community values were stressed, as in the arguments of Hobbes and Rousseau, the ultimate object was still the welfare of each individual citizen as opposed to some collective goal. Furthermore, the average citizen was assumed in all cases to possess the capacity to judge rationally which types of governmental institutions, policies and leaders would best serve his interests.

The critiques reviewed in this chapter attack the liberal position by questioning its assumptions of the primacy of the interests of the individual over those of the community and the primacy of reason over sentiments or obligations as motivations for human behaviour. In addition there are critiques which attack the institutional arrangements of governments favoured by liberal democrats or the economic arrangements of society, especially the status of private property, associated with liberal democracy.

2

The Importance of Community: Edmund Burke. The British statesman and philosopher, Edmund Burke (1729–1797), had less faith in the rationality of individual citizens than he had in the collective wisdom embodied in the traditions of a nation's institutions. Such traditions were in his view more than the mere product of reason; they resulted from the non-rational sentiments, inclinations and prejudices of men as well.

In spite of Hume's arguments to the contrary, Burke viewed the state as the product of a contract. But this was a contract of far greater importance 'than a partnership agreement in a trade of pepper and coffee, calico and tobacco, or some other such low concern ...' It was not to be dissolved for utilitarian reasons 'at the fancy of the parties'.[1] The long-standing institutions of government reflected the traditions of society and gave meaning to men's lives. As Aristotle had said, society was a necessity: '... the man who lives wholly detached from others must be either an angel or a devil.'[2]

It followed that institutions of long standing had a presumptive right to continue to exist. Social institutions should be treated gingerly like a delicate floral arrangement. Social change or reform was indeed possible, at times even desirable, but such reform should proceed with the utmost care, lest the delicate bouquet of existing institutions be destroyed in the process. Reform, therefore, did not fall within the purview of ordinary citizens. Rather, it was a considered task to be undertaken by skilled politicians who understood the significance of the existing order of society.

In terms of practical politics Burke's philosophy led him to support the American Revolution of 1776 but to condemn the French Revolution of 1789. In his view the American Revolution, like the Glorious Revolution of 1688, harkened back to the ancient rights and privileges of British subjects. The revolutionaries were intent upon reclaiming their violated 'chartered rights', rights whose recognition dated back as far as the Magna Carta. In contrast the French revolutionaries sought not to re-establish ancient rights or even to reform existing practices. They sought to destroy utterly the existing order and to build a new one from scratch. Burke viewed this as an impossible foolish undertaking, one that would (and did) lead ultimately to disaster and chaos.

Consistent with his principles, Burke argued that as a Member of Parliament he owed his constituents his best judgement as to what would truly serve their interests. He did not feel bound by their opinions, for he was elected as a Member of Parliament not as a member *from* Bristol.[3] His constituents should judge him periodically, but on the basis of his overall performance, not on the basis of his stand on one particular issue.

45

What emerges from Burke is a fundamental distrust in the ability of each man to reason out the best policy for himself and the community. Yet as a remedy Burke did not propose wedding each citizen's will with the interests of the community as Rousseau did with the ill-defined general will. What is required, Burke contended, is a coterie of leaders who can place the interest of individual citizens into the broader perspective of the interests of the community. The community itself reflects the wisdom and the sentiments of generations of mankind. It lends meaning to men's present existence, and its institutions are not to be trifled with. 'I feel an insuperable reluctance in giving my hand to destroy any established institution of government, upon a theory, however plausible it may be,' Burke said.[4]

3

The Reaction to Hume: Kant and Hegel. The German philosopher, Immanuel Kant (1724–1804), believed Hume was correct in pointing out the differences between statements of cause and effect and statements of morality and rights. Reason alone could tell us nothing about the former; observation alone can tell us nothing about the latter. But Kant did not want to go as far as Hume in stating that morality and rights were merely matters of convention, susceptible to neither logical nor empirical proof. Instead he proposed an ethical theory with implications for politics through which he sought to combine empirical observation with *a priori* reasoning.

On what should men base their actions if not upon natural law and natural rights? Kant answered that actions should be based upon good will. Even though reason could not tell men what actually was good, reason could still be used to consider the *idea* of something being good. Kant proposed that men translate good will into action by following what he called the 'categorical imperative': never take any moral action unless that action could be adopted to a universal rule for human conduct.[5]

But how do we determine that an action can serve as a universal rule for human conduct? Such a determination requires empirical observation and assessment of the consequence of the action. Thus empirical observation must be added to pure reason before the reasoning itself becomes a useful guide for behaviour.

Arguing in a parallel fashion, Kant pointed out that the laws of natural science did not emerge from random observations of correlated phenomena. The selection of things to observe was narrowed through the use of reason. In short for both morality and natural science, neither reason nor observation alone was sufficient. Both were needed: concepts without precepts were empty; precepts without concepts were blind.[6]

Kant's political theory was an application of his ethical theory to the governing of men. For Kant the state existed in order to promote freedom in accordance with universal law. But, as his ethical theory demonstrated, no one could recognize for certain just what was a universal law. The solution was to promulgate laws which were based, insofar as possible, upon the precepts of the categorical imperative. Furthermore the fundamental law or institution of the state ought to reflect the collective (good) will of the people. When these conditions were met, then citizens would have a moral obligation or duty to obey the law, for the law would represent an expression of their collective will. Like Rousseau's citizens, the citizens of Kant's state in effect obeyed no one but themselves when they fulfilled the duties imposed by law.

The state, for Kant, was more than an institutional arrangement based upon utility. It was an approximation to the moral order of nature, and men were obligated to obey this order, even though they could not fully comprehend it.

Where Kant tried to reconcile pure reason with empirical observation Georg Wilhelm Friedrich Hegel (1770–1831) placed pure reason in the dominant position. In his *Philosophy of History*, published (posthumously) in 1832, he suggested that history itself was nothing more than the unfolding of divine reason. Men could try to understand this reason; they could delay or hinder its advance; but they could neither stop nor change it. History used the passions, the instincts, and the intelligence of man to achieve its divine purposes, purposes of which men were mostly unaware. In this way history combined freedom and necessity.

Traditional natural law was rejected by Hegel but so too was Hume. Hegel believed that absolute values and absolute truths of divine reason manifested themselves in social institutions, but only partially. Our knowledge of these absolutes grows by a process Hegel called 'dialectic'. Men holding certain value positions will recognize partial manifestations of divine reason, and they will seek to justify, promote, and protect them. This position Hegel called 'thesis'. Other men sharing different values will point out the faults in the thesis. This position Hegel called 'antithesis'. The clash of the two positions resulted in a third and higher position, the 'synthesis', which contained more recognition of divine reason than either the thesis or its antithesis. It should be emphasized that the synthesis is a *new* position; it is more than a mere compromise or combination of the previous positions. In turn the synthesis becomes the new thesis, and the dialectic process repeats itself, each time revealing more and more of the absolute values and absolute truths.

The state was the instrument through which history was enacted. It was not the creation of individual wills, but the actualization of divine reason. As such, the state transcended individuals' purposes: it included not only the individual citizens of today, but those of the past and of the future. Occupying this exalted position it commanded the unquestioning obedience of the citizenry.

Contrary to Kant's argument, each citizen was not entitled to individual consideration on the basis of his humanity. Instead each citizen must subordinate his own personal interests to those of the state. In doing so the citizen achieved true freedom and true self-realization, for he became a participant in God's great plan of history.

For the purposes of our discussion, the details of Hegel's philosophy are of less importance than its influence. His view of the state as the instrument of divine reason, and his subordination of the vulgar interests of the individual to this divine reason were taken up and expanded upon a century later by fascist critics of liberal democracy. More immediately, his dialectical method was adopted by Marx in order to explain the inevitability of the triumph of communism over bourgeois liberalism.

4

Socialist Critiques of Liberal Democracy. For better or for worse liberal democracy grew up in countries with capitalist economies. Its major nineteenth-century spokesmen – the English utilitarians – generally accepted Adam Smith's argument that *laissez-faire* capitalism brought the maximum amount of prosperity to citizens.[7] The utilitarians were willing to consider an active role for government in the fields like international diplomacy, colonial administration, criminal law, public health and sanitation, but in the economy they reduced government's role to that of enforcing contracts and protecting private property. In the latter half of the century a group of extreme liberals, who became known as 'Social Darwinists', pushed the argument somewhat further. Their most influential spokesman was the English engineer, journalist and social philsopher Herbert Spencer (1820–1903).

Spencer loved liberty so much that he wished to reduce government's role to an absolute minimum. He argued that each citizen must have virtually absolute freedom to compete with his fellow citizens. The only limits were that the competition should be fair and open – more or less refereed by government – and that the accumulated fruits of victory – private property – be protected by the government. The results of such fair competition inevitably led to a differential in rewards, but a fair one nevertheless. The fittest would survive; the weak would succumb.[8] And in Spencer's view this accorded with the laws of nature, which governed men and other biological species.

Furthermore, when Spencer asserted government's role should be minimal, he really meant minimal. Government should not provide poor relief, public education, public sanitation, postal services or even a monetary system. All such services interfered with a citizen's personal liberty: either they forced payment of taxes for services the citizen might not desire, or they prevented the offer of services by private entrepreneurs, which the citizen might otherwise accept. Besides, Spencer argued, once government started providing public services, there was no definite point at which it could stop. For instance, if the state became responsible for educating children (as John Stuart Mill would suggest), then why should it not also become responsible for feeding and clothing them? To Spencer such a responsibility seemed utterly preposterous for the state to assume.

The immediate implications of Spencer's arguments were that in countries claiming to be democracies, those who had managed to accumulate great wealth simply deserved their riches; and those who had nothing equally deserved their fate. The status of the former proved they were superior beings, fit to survive. The status of the latter was their badge of inferiority. They were doomed to perish. For the state to help these inferior citizens not only interfered with the liberties of their more deserving brethren. It contravened the harsh law of nature – that only the fittest shall survive.

Social Darwinism gained its greatest popularity in the United States, where it proved particularly well suited to the young country which boasted both a claim of great economic opportunity for all and a coterie of successful entrepreneurs who accumulated capital regardless of the costs to others. And in spite of our supposed acceptance of the welfare state, Spencerian arguments remain with us today. Who has not heard about how his tax money is wasted on programmes which benefit the undeserving – usually the poor? Oh, how much better off we would be, if only we were at liberty to spend that money privately on whatever we chose!

In contrast to orthodox liberal democrats nineteenth-century socialists were more concerned with the distribution of wealth than with the opportunity to accumulate it. Where liberal democrats accepted a social order which still had sharp divisions between the rich and the poor, between areas of scarcity and areas of abundance, their socialist critics argued that for the first time in history society had the economic capabilities to provide a materially satisfactory life for every citizen. These socialist arguments fell roughly into two categories: (1) the Utopian, which provided great detail about the characteristics of the desired social order, but presented little detail about how to achieve it and (2) the scientific, which explained how to bring about a new social order, but gave only basic details of its characteristics.

Father of the nineteenth-century Utopian socialists was the Frenchman, Henri Saint-Simon (1760–1825). Saint-Simon differed from his contemporaries in that he placed modern science and technology in the forefront of his political philosophy. For Saint-Simon, discussion of liberty or equality in the abstract meant little. Industry, not a paper constitution, was the true cornerstone of liberty, for industry had the unprecedented power to produce goods to be used for the betterment of mankind. Traditional political leadership should be replaced by scientific elites who understood this new industrial capacity and could plan accordingly.

Saint-Simon viewed the established church, the French monarchy, and the landed gentry as drones, living off the largesse of industry, but contributing nothing to it. He argued that social rewards should be based upon abilities and contributions to society, rather than upon possession of titles or riches. After all, he pointed out, if the drones were to disappear, there might be regret, but life would continue much as before. If on the other hand the scientists disappeared, France (or any modern country) would rapidly be reduced to a third rate power.

In his *Letters from a Citizen of Geneva* (1803) Saint-Simon presented a vision of a society led by an executive council of enlightened scientists and industrialists. In this new society private property would remain, but its ownership would be distributed more fairly and, when necessary, the government would extend, curtail, or otherwise regulate the use of private property. Saint-Simon thought that the executive council could secure the cooperation of both rich financiers and ordinary workers in order to achieve its purpose. To facilitate this cooperation he proposed a legislature of three houses, to which representatives were elected on the basis of occupation rather than domicile. Nor did Saint-Simon neglect the spiritual needs of the community. He outlined a new sort of Christianity, more optimistic than the old, which held that material prosperity was a prerequisite for spiritual development.[9]

The Utopians who followed Saint-Simon gradually became full-fledged socialists. As the century progressed, most came to view private property as a hindrance to the material well-being of the ordinary citizen, and called, therefore, for its abolition. They developed and modified Saint-Simon's original ideas, tending to favour more decentralized and less elite forms of government. The best known of these Utopian socialists were the Frenchmen, Charles Fourier (1772–1837) and Pierre Proudhon (1809–1865), and the Welshman, Robert Owen (1771–1858).

From our present day perspective Fourier's ideas seem somewhat fantastic. Fourier proposed establishing a few ideal communities called phalanxes, which would serve as model communities for others to imitate. Among other things these phalanxes, which Fourier described in amazing detail, were to consist of 1500 to 1600 people, were to occupy 500 acres, and were to be economically self-sufficient. The important features of Fourier's communities, however, were that their economies were based upon the principle of social cooperation rather than free competition, and that their modes of operation were designed to appeal more to men's passions than to their reason.

Fourier postulated the principle of 'passional attraction' as a God-given universal law of human behaviour. His communities were designed to create harmonious relationships among their citizens by offering a wide variety of constructive outlets for their diverse passions. He believed that through properly planned systems of remuneration the various types of work required could be made attractive to different sub-groups of citizens. All rewards and statuses were not to be the same. Capital, labour and talent were to be awarded different rates of pay. Moreover, Fourier argued that some disparities in status were good for the community, for they provided incentives for more productive work and they encouraged union by increasing citizens' mutual curiosity about one another.

The ideas of Robert Owen resembled those of Fourier in many ways, but they tended to be more practical, for Owen also spent most of his life trying to implement them. He was a self-made businessman whose early successes had convinced him that enlightened treatment of workers not only increased their happiness, it also increased their productivity. His outstanding achievement was the successful operation of the model industrial village of New Lanark, whose factories he inherited in the early 1800s from his father-in-law who had founded the village. In New Lanark Owen practised a benevolent paternalism. Factory conditions were clean and sanitary; factory hours were relatively short; child labour was curtailed. The village housing was attractive, and free education was provided for all children. Educational and recreational facilities were made available for adults as well. Under his enlightened tutelage the village and Owen himself prospered. He reported on his successes and speculated on the more general application of his business methods in *A New View of Society* (1814) and *Report on the County of Lanark* (1821).

His thought advanced from paternalistic capitalism to planned communal villages. He envisioned communities of some 800 to 1200 persons sharing common kitchen and dining facilities, but living in family units in centrally heated apartments. Communal life would be organized around the factory, although some agricultural fields would be maintained on the village's 800 or so acres. Children would be educated on a similar basis as that practised in New Lanark, and similar civic amenities would also be provided. But the village would do its own planning, mostly by boards of directors composed of more elderly and experienced citizens.

In the 1820s he went to the United States to help found the village of New Harmony. This village was set up on a communal self-governing basis, and was far grander in scale – 30,000 acres – and more agricultural than Owen had previously envisaged. In its short existence it went through six new constitutions, enjoyed multifarious cultural activities, but, sadly, it grew few crops. Owen lost his shirt and returned to England. He was not disheartened, however. In the 1830s and 40s he played important, though not spectacularly successful, roles in organizing the trade-union movement and in setting up Rochdale-type consumer cooperatives.

Owen believed that labour was the source of all wealth and that environment moulded human character. When employers did not follow his example by providing a healthy work environment for labour, the source of their wealth, Owen tried to set up his own colonies. When these failed, he turned to labour union organizations to improve wages and conditions. He also lobbied Parliament for legislation to improve industrial working conditions.

Of the Utopian socialists we have mentioned, Proudhon was perhaps the most radical. In *What is Property?* (1840) he put forward the simple, yet startling assertion that property was robbery, plain and simple. Why was property robbery? Because it represented the exploitation of those who worked by those who did not work. Labour created everything of economic value, and the labourer properly was entitled to the full fruits of his labour, once production costs were deducted. Under the system of property ownership, however, those who held property, whether land or capital, were able to appropriate for themselves most of the value created by those who laboured under their auspices. Hence property amounted to robbery.

The way to end this robbery of course was to eliminate property. But Proudhon did not favour communistic-type solutions like those Robert Owen had come to favour, in which the rewards were the same for each, regardless of each citizen's contribution to the community. Equal remuneration led to exploitation of the strong and industrious citizens by the weak and the lazy. Proudhon favoured instead the creation of small, self-sufficient syndicates, underwritten by a mutually supported free credit bank, each governed scientifically by a department of statistics, which would remunerate citizens in proportion to the value of their contributions to the community. Proudhon believed that such syndicates would eliminate the authority of man over man and would substitute the authority of science in its place. He called this form of government 'anarchy', and he viewed it as the mark of a mature society.

In retrospect the Utopian socialists emerge as humanistic reformers concerned with organizing society in such a manner that each citizen is free to improve himself. They recognized the obstacles to self-improvement which the capitalist system imposed, but they believed that these could be overcome through a spirit of cooperation between all classes of citizens. Their elaborate plans for future societies revealed a certain distrust for the political judgements of the ordinary citizens. Government usually was to be administered by scientific elites, whose planning would be based upon what science revealed was good for society, not upon what citizens happened to think was good at the moment. Their penchant for small-scale communities, however, served to limit the governing powers of even the scientific elites. Once social institutions were properly arranged, they expected government's role to be minimal. They favoured an administration of things – scientifically designed laws and procedures – in place of an administration of men.

The giants of scientific socialism were Karl Marx (1818–83) and his friend and collaborator Friedrich Engels (1820–95). Both were German by birth, but they lived most of their productive years in England. As mentioned above their objections to liberal democracy's attachment to capitalism did not differ fundamentally from those of the Utopians, but in comparison to the Utopians they spent far more time considering how a socialist society would be achieved and far less time considering the details of just what this socialist society would look like.

As a young man educated in Germany, Marx came under the influence of Hegelian dialectic as a method of studying history. He developed a keen appreciation of the insights to be gained from viewing history as a dynamic process as indicated by the dialectic. But he did not accept that the unfolding of history was the unfolding of a divine idea. Indeed it was the other way around: the material conditions of our history determined our ideas including even our ideas of the divine. In 1845 he and Engels wrote:

In direct contrast to German philosophy, which descends from heaven to earth, here we ascend from earth to heaven ... Morality, religion, metaphysics, all the rest of ideology and their corresponding forms of consciousness, thus no longer retain the semblance of independence. They have no history, no development; but men, developing their material production and their material intercourse, alter, along with this, their real existence, their thinking, and the products of their thinking. Life is not determined by consciousness, but consciousness by life. In the first [German-Hegelian] method of approach the starting point is consciousness taken as the living individual; in the second it is the real, living individuals themselves, as they are in actual life, and consciousness is considered solely as *their* consciousness.[10]

They dubbed their new method of studying history 'dialectical materialism'. Having thus 'turned Hegel on his head' Marx and Engels still needed to identify the materialistic theses and antitheses implied by their dialectics. To this end they depicted social classes as the vehicles through which history was enacted. A person's class was determined by his relationship to the means of production in his society, and over different periods of history different distributions of social classes could be found. Moreover, between any two periods of history the relative importance of the social classes varied.

In the nineteenth century Marx and Engels surmised that the capitalist class, the bourgeoisie, was dominant. It was opposed by its antithesis, the working class or proletariat. In the previous historical period – feudalism – the dominant classes had been lords, vassals and guild masters. Their antitheses were journeymen, apprentices and serfs. The bourgeoisie, who were to form the new synthesis, first appeared as merchants and traders in the market towns and chartered burghs. With the discovery of the New World and the opening of trade routes to the Far East industry and commerce were provided with unprecedented opportunities and incentives for expansion. The bourgeoisie responded to the new markets, but the feudal classes could not adjust. With the inventions of modern industrial machinery at their disposal to provide for ever increasing productive capacity, the bourgeoisie emerged as the dominant class, and the feudal system collapsed. The bourgeois period of history had begun.

But bourgeois society contained its own contradictions. With industrialization emerged a new class, the proletariat. The proletariat differed from other historical classes in that it had no economic rights or privileges. Each member of the proletariat must sell his labour to the bourgeois property owners in return for a wage. A proletarian, unlike even the lowliest serf, had no share whatsoever in the product he created.

Here was where bourgeois liberal democracy went awry. For man was a tool-making animal: he achieved his self-expression and fulfilment through fashioning tools and using them to create products. But under the bourgeois economic system – capitalism – the capitalist appropriated the worker's product for himself. By doing so the capitalist not only robbed the proletarian of his product, he robbed him of his soul. The worker under the capitalist system thus became 'alienated' from himself.

It did no good for liberal democrats to point to political rights and liberties which by now were gaining wide acceptance among the rapidly industrializing nations of Europe and North America. Such rights and liberties were really illusionary, for they served mostly to protect property, not people. In fact as far as most ordinary citizens, i.e. the proletarians were concerned, the whole political process was basically a sham. Political institutions, government, politics – they all reflected the material relations of production, the economic system over which the bourgeoisie ruled supreme. Government was nothing more than the executive committee of the bourgeoisie. Politics itself was superstructure; the underlying economic relations were fundamental in determining the character of politics.

How could alienation be eliminated? How could the citizen recover his true freedom of self-expression? If not by ordinary politics then how?

By revolution, Marx and Engels answered. By a revolution which overthrew the bourgeoisie by fundamentally altering the relations of production. The proletariat, who greatly outnumbered the bourgeoisie, would seize the property. They would expropriate those who had previously been the expropriators, and they would establish a dictatorship of the proletariat. This dictatorship would not be the new historical synthesis, however. It was still politics as usual, but with one significant difference. For the first time the majority, the proletariat in this case, would have control of the government. They would oppress the minority, the bourgeoisie, instead of the minority oppressing them.

The dictatorship of the proletariat was to be a transitory stage. After the bourgeoisie had been eliminated, the state would progress to the new synthesis – the communist society. In this society government would wither away. As the Utopians had envisaged, an administration of things would replace an administration of men. Citizens would be free to develop their talents to the fullest extent: communal ownership of property and the products of labour would eliminate alienation, the chief obstacle to such development. This, not bourgeois society, was a true democracy.

Marx and Engels spent relatively little time describing the communist society they hoped to create. They spent a great deal of time developing an economic theory which buttressed their dialectic interpretation. For our purposes, details of the theory are less important than its predictions.[11] It predicted ever-increasing numbers of proletarians living and working in ever-increasing misery, continually exploited by fewer and more powerful bourgeois capitalists. The capitalists had no choice in the matter; in order to compete with their rivals they had to squeeze every drop of surplus value (the difference between the market value of a product and the cost it takes to produce it, including the wage of the worker) they could from the worker. The economic trends would inexorably lead to a situation ripe for a confrontation between proletariat and bourgeoisie. All that was needed then were a few leaders to help the proletariat develop a class consciousness, a realization of the commonality of the cause of all working peoples, and the revolution would follow:

> The Communists disdain to conceal their view and aims. They openly declare that their ends can be attained only by the forcible overthrow of all existing social conditions. Let the ruling classes tremble at a Communist revolution. The proletarians have nothing to lose but their chains. They have a world to win. Working men of all countries, unite! [12]

The communist revolution leads to the dictatorship of the proletariat. This in turn gives way to the communist society, the new synthesis. What new historical stages follow next?

For this question Marx and Engels provided a slick answer. The communist society they pointed out is a classless society. Since there are no owners or masters, there are no oppressed classes either. Everyone contributes to the welfare of the society as best he can. In return everyone has the same privileges, and everyone is entitled to the same rewards. But it will be recalled that classes are the vehicles through which dialectical materialism proceeds. When classes disappear, the dialectic process comes to a halt. The communist society is the final synthesis; it is the last stage of history. There are no fundamental historical changes to follow. History, so to speak, has come to an end.

Together the socialist critiques emphasized that there could be no true equality of opportunity, no true exercise of freedom, without a fundamental redistribution of property, or better still, its total elimination. The political rights and privileges of liberal democracy were empty as far as the bulk of the citizenry were concerned. They served to protect property rights and hence to justify the capitalist's appropriation of the products of the worker, the removal of his self-expression. The worker must regain control of these fruits of his labours before there could be any real democracy.

The Utopians hoped to achieve a voluntary transformation of society through reform based upon their educating the populace, especially the scientific and industrial elites, to the merits of their case. The scientific socialists entertained no such pleasant hopes for reform. They saw class antagonisms which only a revolution could eliminate. In the end scientific socialism made the greater impact. The work of Marx and Engels inspired the formation of international workingmen's movements and of socialist and communist political parties on the European continent and in the United States. The greatest triumph for scientific socialism came with the Russian Revolution, whose leader, Vladimir I. Lenin (1870–1924), derived his ideas directly from Marx and Engels.[13]

5

The attack on representative institutions. Although they differed in their specific composition and in the specific powers they controlled, the political institutions of liberal-democratic countries were essentially similar. They consisted of an executive branch of government, the head of which normally was indirectly elected by the people; a legislative branch, often bicameral, at least one house of which was elected directly by the people; and a judiciary, the members of which were generally appointed by the executive but remained independent by holding office for far longer terms than the executive official who appointed them.[14]

This combination of political institutions was called 'republican' or 'representative' government, and it was strongly defended by liberals of great stature, such as James Madison (1751–1836), fourth President of the United States and major architect of its Constitution, and John Stuart Mill, the great philosopher and scholar, whom we have already discusssed.

Among other things, Madison and Mill pointed out three major advantages of representative government: (1) it provided a means for governing large populations scattered over vast expanses of territory, in contrast to the limited populations and city-state-like territories required for direct citizen participation; (2) in a liberal society where status is achieved on the basis of merit it was likely that the citizens' representatives, an elected elite, would be of above average ability; (3) as citizens would be likely to vote for representatives who tended to hold beliefs and opinions similar to their own, representative government provided an excellent means of implementing popular sovereignty. Mill even went so far as to argue that of all contemporary forms of government, representative government was 'the ideally best polity'.[15]

Needless to say, not everyone bought such optimistic conclusions. Implicit in the socialist critique of liberal democracy was a distrust of representative government. Neither the Utopians nor the Marxists included representative institutions in their ideal states. The Utopians favoured government by scientific and industrial elites or virtually no government at all. Marxists favoured a withering away of strong government once the transition period of dictatorship of the proletariat had been completed, and to the extent that collective decisions were necessary in a communist state, they seemed to favour direct rather than representative participation by citizens.

Rousseau had preceded the socialists in citing objections to representative institutions. In order for the will of each citizen to achieve harmony with the general will Rousseau recommended direct rather than representative democracy. Citizen participation bred citizen responsibility; direct participation was the mark of a good government. Conversely, lack of direct participation implied a bad government with a citizenry either politically apathetic or absorbed only in satisfying their own selfish wills. In Rousseau's view electing representatives merely produced an excuse for citizens not to pay attention to politics. It bred apathy, and it invited the destruction of liberty:

> As soon as public service ceases to be the main business of citizens, and they prefer to serve with their purses rather than with their persons, the state is already on the brink of ruin. Is it necessary to go forth to war? They hire troops and remain at home. Is it necessary to take counsel? They appoint deputies and remain at home. By dint of laziness and money, they end up by having mercenaries to enslave their country, and representatives to sell it.[16]

He went on to argue that the general will could not be represented anyway. Either it belonged to all citizens or it did not; there was no intermediate possibility. He felt that representatives of the people could act as instructed delegates only. Any law which so-called representatives passed, if it did not already accord with their binding instructions, had to be ratified by all the people before it could be accepted as valid. Representative government, such as that of England, really amounted to nothing more than slavery. The English were free only when they were electing Members of Parliament. Between elections they were enslaved because their representatives could pass laws which were binding upon them without seeking their prior approval.

Rousseau recognized that direct citizen participation implied that the state had to be rather limited in size and territory. He frankly preferred confederations of small autonomous governmental units to the formation of one large government for a territory. This too was a position favoured by the Utopian socialists.

Where Rousseau argued that legislative assemblies could not represent the general will, the Guild Socialists argued that such assemblies misrepresented it. Writing in the early decades of the twentieth century, they claimed that the only sensible basis for representation was function, not territory. A modern legislator who invariably represented a large territorial constituency, could not possibly reflect the diverse political interests and opinions of his constituents. But if his constituents were drawn only from those who performed the same function in society, say, actors, lorry drivers, or steel workers, then there was a fair probability that he could discover and represent their common interests and opinions. Mainly comprised of middle-class intellectuals, the Guild Socialists never could quite agree upon just how the government they desired would be organized, but the ideas of G. D. H. Cole, (1889–1959) their best known spokesman (though he later recanted), are representative of their main lines of thought.[17]

Cole envisaged a government comprised at its core by a series of autonomous producers' guilds. These guilds would be formed originally from industry-wide unions, and they would be responsible for the planning and management of production in their segments of the economy. Capital would be collectivized, but it would be under the control of the guilds instead of a central state. With their own guilds as employers, workers would achieve a status and dignity unknown under the wage slavery of private capitalism or socialism's nationalized industries (state capitalism).

Members of guilds would elect their own legislatures and executives, and these in turn would select representatives to serve on a joint council composed of members of all important guilds. This joint council would coordinate the planning efforts of the separate guilds, and would adjudicate disputes, should they arise, but it would not legislate as would an ordinary parliament.

The state would not disappear, but it would lose its sovereign status. It would remain a territorial association, but would represent citizens only in their capacities as consumers. (Consumer representatives would also serve on the joint council.) In addition to producer guilds and the consumer association there would be a multiplicity of self-governing associational groups representing other interests or functions in society. The general rule would be not 'one man, one vote' but 'one man as many votes as interests, but only one vote in relation to each interest'.[18]

Although the objections Rousseau and the Guild Socialists raised to the systems of representation employed by liberal-democratic governments have never deterred the operations of such institutions, a number of recent developments indicate governments are moving towards overcoming them. Recent trends towards devolution, home rule, community control and the like are usually rationalized in terms of giving citizens more control over local resources in order to solve community problems – a development which would gladden Rousseau (were he still around to be gladdened). And the burgeoning of planning boards with representatives drawn from labour, industry or other relevant sectors of the population can be interpreted as a belated recognition that functional representation is necessary to supplement the scheme of territorial representation, with which Anglo-American governments have traditionally operated.

6

Anarchism. From socialist notions that property is robbery and that the state supports property, it is but a small step to the conclusion that elimination of the state, rather than elimination of property, should come first on the agenda of the reformer (or revolutionary). This is precisely the conclusion that the radical anarchist, Michael Bakunin (1814–76), tried to impose upon the (First) International Workingmen's Association, the international movement which Marx helped found in 1864. Not only was Bakunin ready to attack the state first, he was ready to do it now in a spontaneous, unplanned fashion. Once the state was destroyed, he expected that things would get sorted out, for he believed that men's natural inclinations to cooperate would immediately come to the fore.

Needless to say, Marx, who counted on using existing government bureaucracy after the revolution to consolidate the position of the proletariat, was not at all pleased with the tactics of Bakunin and his followers. (Marx had previously crossed swords – or pens anyway – with Proudhon over similar matters.) Their dispute dominated the internal politics of the International and climaxed with the expulsion of the Bakunin factions by the Hague Congress of the International in 1872. To avoid further conflict with Bakunin's supporters, who still remained influential in some European working-class movements (*e.g.* in Switzerland and Spain), Marx transferred the headquarters of the International to the United States, where the organization finally died in 1876.

The anarchist challenge to Marx's scientific socialism did not disappear, however. Where Proudhon and Bakunin had been extravagant and combative in their denunciations and their claims, the Russian exile, Prince Peter Kropotkin (1842–1921), developed a gentle and seductive argument for anarchism, which, despite its overwhelming optimism about men's conduct, remains the clearest, best-reasoned case ever made for the elimination of the central power of the state.[19]

Kropotkin's logic rested upon the conviction that Darwin's message of survival of the fittest meant not survival of the strongest, but survival of those species best able to adapt to changing environmental circumstances. Those species which proved best able to adapt were more often than not those who relied upon cooperation and mutual aid rather than competition with members of their own species. Man's survival indicated he was such an adaptable creature. Society, therefore, could be organized to take advantage of men's natural proclivity to cooperate. Kropotkin thought, as had the Utopian socialists, that the appeal of his ideas could stimulate a virtually bloodless revolution, in which all classes would cooperate.

In outline the self-sufficient communes which Kropotkin envisaged are already familiar to us, for they differed little from those of Proudhon, Bakunin, or Owen. Kropotkin favoured a complete communal basis for remuneration: to each according to his needs as opposed to to each according to his contribution. And Kropotkin favoured free negotiations between communes and even between sub-groups within the communes to provide the basis of order. What really distinguished Kropotkin from his intellectual predecessors, however, was the practicality of his economics. As an agricultural expert who also had a keen appreciation of the capacities of early twentieth-century technology, he detailed plans of how the communes could develop viable economies in varying environmental circumstance. If Kropotkin was unrealistic in his estimates of men's good will and cooperative spirit, he was nonetheless convincing that if men could be induced to cooperate, the communes he envisaged were viable.

7

Elites. Gaetano Mosca (1858–1941), Italian philosopher and statesman, lived long enough to see his criticisms of democratic political institutions vindicated and yet to feel remorse over the fact that to a large extent he had been correct. Mosca's *The Ruling Class*, first published in 1890, contained the assertion that in every society, even so-called democracies, the real governing is done not by the people but by a political class.

The political class were not necessarily an economic class, Marx notwithstanding, but they were decidedly not the majority. The political class ruled by a political formula, a myth designed to justify their position of political power. The myth might be a democratic or an aristocratic justification, but in any case, it must be tailored generally to fit the political traditions of the society in order to provide the moral force needed to extract obedience to and deference for the elite political class.

The elite never 'represented' the people. Even at election times the citizens were presented not with a broad choice of alternative policies but with a meagre selection of two or three parties or candidates, the nominations of which were effectively out of their control. Nor was revolution an answer. In modern times the state had such a monopoly of force that the only successful revolutions were palace revolutions, *coups d'état* through which one faction of the elite displaced another.

Mosca was not particularly happy about the inevitable emergence of a political elite. He considered that his conclusions for better or for worse, were the result of his scientific analysis of social relations. Even though he was never an enthusiastic democrat – he looked upon popular elections as vulgar auctions in which competing elites in their bids for votes made promises appealing to the masses' worst instincts – he nonetheless preferred democratic elections to Mussolini's fascism, and he served as a democratically elected deputy in the pre-fascist Italian parliament. His own preference was for open political competition among elites led by sensible men with middle-class virtues, men not unlike Mosca himself.[20]

The late nineteenth and early twentieth centuries saw the rise of

65

mass-based socialist parties in Europe, political organizations which Mosca had not specifically taken into account in his analysis. These parties had as their roots local cells, members of whom had some control over selection of party officers, adoption of candidates, and development of party policy. Perhaps this type of mass party made it possible for the average citizen of a large and populous state to participate in politics so effectively that a political class could not exert control.

Not so, said Robert Michels, (1876–1936) in his book, *Political Parties*, first published in 1911. To be effective, a political party, even a socialist one, could not be a democratic organization. A party needed to find and to keep candidates committed to its programme. If it did not hold a majority of seats, it would need to bargain and compromise with opposition parties. The party also had to plan election strategy, raise finances, and maintain its internal bureaucracy. For these and similar tasks discipline and unity of command were far more effective than participatory democracy by the rank and file.

Anyway, the hard fact was that the average rank and file party member did not give a damn about party affairs and consequently paid little attention to party organization. Party officials, on the other hand, cared a great deal about the affairs of the party. After a time these officials became professionalized. They severed their connections with outside employers and began to receive their entire support from salaries drawn from the party coffers. This professionalization served only to consolidate the party leadership's desire to remain in party office, for now a return to their former employment would mean a demotion in both status and pay. The upshot of all this was that the party ceased to be an organization with a purpose. It became instead a vehicle for maintaining the privileges of a few:

> Not merely does the party sacrifice its political virginity, by entering into promiscuous relationships with the most heterogeneous of political elements, ... it exposes itself in addition to the risk of losing its essential character of a party.[21]

As an elite emerged within political parties, so an elite emerged within any large collectivity. Michels postulated the 'iron law of oligarchy': every organization complex enough to require a division of labour creates for itself sub-groups which, as soon as they become consolidated, begin to pursue interests peculiar to themselves, interests which may be contrary to the collective interests of members of the organization. Socialist parties might conquer bourgeois elites, but socialism would not triumph. Socialism would perish with socialists' ascension to power. Once instituted, Marx's dictatorship of the proletariat would never end.

Michels, who explicitly acknowledged his intellectual debt to Mosca, believed along with his master that free competition among elites was the best sort of government one could hope for.

8

Conclusions: In spite of the attacks upon it liberal democracy emerged from the nineteenth century as the dominant political philosophy in Western Europe and North America. With the first two decades of the new century came the final demise of the powers of hereditary political institutions, such as the House of Lords, the Kaiser, and the Austrian Emperor. In the United States the Senate became subject to direct popular election, and the primary election system brought even nominations of candidates into the hands of the people. By the end of the third decade virtually all barriers to universal adult suffrage had been removed.

Not that the ideas of liberal democrats remained as rigid, unchanging dogma. Indeed they were adjusted to meet the challenges put to them. By the mid-nineteenth century John Stuart Mill had already come to believe that complete *laissez-faire* was incompatible with the aims of liberal democracy. At the very least government had to provide public education, protection of minors and incompetents, protection from contracts binding persons in perpetuity, protection of stockholders from exploitation by management and, in general, protections and services which private individuals would not perform.[22] Mill's list of protections and services grew very large, and towards the end of his life he came to regard himself as a socialist. Picking up where Mill left off the Fabian Society pressed a view that socialism could be brought about through progressive education of the electorate. The electorate in turn would instruct their representatives to use existing institutions of government to bring about the gradual transition from a privately owned and managed economy to a public one. The programme of the newly formed British Labour Party was heavily influenced by these ideas.

Thomas H. Green (1836–82) even tried to re-infuse liberal ideas with a sense of community. His posthumously published *Prolegomena to Ethics* (1883) suggested that citizens could only realize their potential through a well-ordered society, which promoted that realization. True freedom was not the absence of restraint, but the actual possibility of self-development. Promoting such a possibility for all citizens represented a common good, and that common good should be the aim of governmental legislation. Regulation of wages and conditions of employment, of child labour, of standards of housing and of public health all became necessary if freedom was to be anything more than a pious wish.

And whilst liberal democrats were becoming more socialist, some socialists like Edward Bernstein (1850–1932) were becoming less militant. Although raised on German-Marxist orthodoxy, Bernstein could not ignore the fact that the middle classes seemed to be growing, not diminishing in number, and that as the twentieth century approached, the lot of the worker was improving, not getting worse. The revolution Marx and Engels had predicted was not around the corner. It was better to face up to this fact, and to work through the ballot for the evolution of a socialist state.[23] Had Bernstein been English he might well have been a Fabian! His main disagreement with Fabian socialism was that it failed to dissolve the state, once public control over the economy had been established.

Liberal democracy survived because its nineteenth-century critics really shared the same kind of vision as its supporters, regarding the sort of society they desired. On this point even as radical a critic as Bakunin sounds not much different from Mill:

[It is necessary] to organise society in such a manner that every man or woman, coming into life, should find approximately equal means for the development of his different faculties and for their utilisation by his work; to organise a society which, making the exploitation of one by another for ever impossible, should allow each one to participate in the enjoyment of social riches (which are never in fact produced by anything but labour) only to the extent to which he will have directly contributed to the production of this wealth by his own labour.[24]

The more deadly attacks on liberal democracy came after 1930. The Great Depression produced millions of converts to fascism, a philosophy (if we choose to dignify it with the term) which held a fundamentally different view of the sort of society desired. And the advent of the scientific study of public opinion and mass voting behaviour gave rise to grave doubts about the capabilities of the average citizen upon whom liberal democrats placed so much reliance. To these more recent critiques of liberal democracy we now turn.

4 · Liberal Democracy in the Twentieth Century

The man of broad common sense, mixing on equal terms with his neighbors, forming a fair unprejudiced judgment on every question, not viewy or pedantic like the man of learning, nor arrogant like the man of wealth, but seeing things in a practical, businesslike, and withal kindly spirit, pursuing happiness in his own way, and willing that everyone else should do so. Such average men make the bulk of the people, and are pretty sure to go right . . .
Lord (James) Bryce, *Modern Democracies*, Macmillan, 1921.

What is genuinely important is not that the will of mankind in the mass should be formulated and made effective at all times and in every case, but simply that means shall be provided for ascertaining and executing it in capital cases – that there shall be no immovable impediment to its execution when, by some prodigy of nature, it takes a coherent and apposite form.
H. L. Mencken, *Notes on Democracy*, Jonathan Cape, 1926.

In the Fascist conception, to be free, means to be no more a slave to one's own passions, ambitions or desires; means to be free to will what is true, and good and just, at all times, in all cases; means, in other words, to realize here in this world the true mission of man . . . According to Fascism, a true, a great spiritual life cannot take place unless the State has risen to a position of pre-eminence in the world of man . . . Liberty, therefore, cannot be concerned with the individual's claims but must find its maximum concern in the fullest expression of the nation's life, and of the state which of such a life is the concrete realization.
Mario Palmieri, *The Philosophy of Fascism*, Fortuny, 1936.

I

The above three characterizations of the role of the average citizen in governing the polity exemplify three major themes of the twentieth century: the liberal democratic, the democratic-elitist, and the fascist. We are already familiar with the liberal democratic. The democratic-elitist and the fascist characterizations represent twentieth-century responses to problems which challenge the empirical assumptions of supporters of liberal democracy.

In this chapter we shall begin by examining the elitist and fascist views of the average citizen's capacity to govern. We shall then compare how well all three views – elitist, fascist and liberal democratic – match the empirical evidence about the average citizen's political behaviour gathered by twentieth-century political scientists. Finally we shall draw out the implications these findings have for the viability of liberal democracy in the last decades of the twentieth century.

2

Man and the State. If mutual interests promote compatibility, Lord Bryce's (1838–1922) Average Man and our own Good Citizen Brown would find they shared similar interests in the problems of their respective communities and their nations, and similar optimistic views concerning the political judgement and capacities of themselves and of their fellow citizens. For each politics would be conducted with the aim of using the state to facilitate the self-expression of every citizen in the freest possible manner.

These stalwarts of liberal democracy would get along less well with H. L. Mencken's average citizens. Mencken (1880–1946) thought Average Man and Good Citizen Brown were in fact rather rare. To his mind the average citizen was a congenital booby, full of petty jealousies and prejudices, incapable of passing sound judgement on most public issues. Far from tolerating a diversity of choices, the average citizen considered the mission of his political life to be the reduction of available political choices to the few alternatives which conformed to his own pedestrian standards.

Mencken was an admitted elitist: 'It is a tragic but inescapable fact that most of the finest fruits of human progress, like all the nobler virtues of men, are the exclusive possession of small minorities, chiefly unpopular and disreputable.'[1] And he looked upon democracy in his native America as little more than an intolerant and persecutionary rule by a puritanical mob: 'This doctrine that a man who stands in contempt of the prevailing ideology has no rights under law is so thoroughly democratic in the United States, it is seldom questioned save by romantic fanatics, robbed of their wits by an uncritical reading of the Fathers.'[2]

But Mencken was a liberal nonetheless. Members of an elite would resemble Average Man and Citizen Brown, for the elite, after all, embodied the liberal virtues. The elite were motivated by concerns for individual liberty, for dignity and honour. They appreciated that true freedom was not the safe but restricted freedom of a trustee in a penitentiary. It was the freedom to make one's own choices for better or for worse, subject only to the caveat that an individual's choices should not unduly restrict the choices of his fellows, a caveat that comes right out of the great liberal work, John Stuart Mill's *On Liberty*.

In contrast a good citizen of a fascist society bears no resemblance to Average Man and Good Citizen Brown. In fact a good fascist citizen is essentially the opposite of a good liberal democrat. Where the liberal democrat wishes to use the state to further the ends of the individual citizens, the fascist wants the state to use the citizens for its own advancement. Where the liberal democrat wants to decide for himself, the fascist wants the state to decide for him. Where the liberal democrat believes that popular sovereignty should serve to limit the scope of political leaders, the fascist believes in unfettered leadership.

Mencken's critique of democracy, though more bitter than most, is nonetheless in the tradition of conservative liberalism. Of the writers we have already discussed, Hobbes, Burke, and Mosca would find that his arguments paralleled their own on many points. Moreover, Mencken's insistence that a genuine aristocracy was needed to create and lead a party of liberty, harkens back as far as the need for a guardian class described in Plato's *Republic* (380 B.C.).

Fascism's critique of liberal democracy sounds less familiar. Only loosely resembling a right wing Hegelianism, fascist philosophy, like Topsy, 'just growed'. For the most part systematic attempts to justify fascism followed, rather than preceded, the ascensions of fascist leaders to power in Italy and Germany. Their basic point is that the subordination of the interests of the individual to those of the state will lead to a just society, one in which the citizen will realize 'true' liberty. Instead of following his own inclinations, as he does under liberal democracy, the citizen subjects his will to a higher one.

The higher will, however, is not the will of Hegel's divine or universal spirit. Far from it. The fascist will arises from the rather parochial spirit of the people, more specifically, of the Italian or German people, depending upon whether we consult an Italian or German fascist philosopher. Furthermore, this will or spirit is not the manifestation of divine reason, nor for that matter of any reason at all. The will of the people is a myth – for the Italian fascists a renewed expression of the glories of the Roman Empire; for the German fascists an expression of racial superiority arising from the true Germanic (Aryan) blood and soil.[3]

Nor does the higher will resemble Rousseau's general will in more than a superficial manner. The citizen's first duty is obedience to this higher will, the concrete expression of which is the fascist state. This higher will is determined not by active participation of all citizens but by the state itself. And what the state commands is in turn determined and promulgated by the fascist leaders, or, when we get down to it, by the authority of *the* leader, Mussolini or Hitler, as it happened. In addition the leader has at his disposal a party to provide the manpower and the muscle for him to enforce his authority.

Liberal democrats and socialists normally envisioned the ideal state as providing each individual with the wherewithal to pursue his own aims and ambitions (giving due consideration to the aims and ambitions of others). The fascist state rises above such crass materialist and selfish concerns. Material prosperity does not necessarily lead to happiness. There are spiritual values as well as economic ones – nationalism and heroism, for example. War for the greater glory of the state calls for exercise of these values and thereby makes a people noble.

Heroism is a primary virtue, but all men are not equally heroic.

The ablest men (who happen to be fascists) must rise to the top. These leaders form an emotional bond with the people. They express the people's innermost hopes.

Not all the aims of fascism can be characterized so nobly. As there are some men who make natural fascist leaders, there are some who cannot be good fascists at all. In both Italy and Germany these outsiders included diehard communists, socialists, and others of the left, but in Germany the Jews were selected as the target group for particular calumny. What marvellous scapegoats the Jews made! Had the government promised farmers high prices and the city-dwellers cheap food? Blame the Jewish middlemen for the failure to achieve these aims. Was there a world-wide economic depression? Blame the Jewish bankers. Were there labour problems? Blame the Jewish communists and unionists. Were there excess profits being made in private industry? Blame the Jewish capitalists:

> While the business agent Moses Cohen persuades his company to react most unfavorably to the demands of the workers, his brother Isaac Cohen, the labor leader, stands in the factory yard, arouses the masses and shouts: just look at them, they only want to oppress you. Throw off your chains! And upstairs his brother sees to it that those chains are well forged.[4]

If all this sounds plainly irrational and not a little mad as we look back on it today, we must keep in mind that millions of people not only accepted these ideas, they killed or were killed for them. And the legacy of scapegoating, in particular, is still with us. Only the scapegoats have changed. These days they tend to be blacks, immigrants or outside agitators instead of Jews.

3

The average citizen in theory: What is the average citizen really like? Is he essentially adrift, in need of discipline and authority, best suited to be a devoted follower, as declared by the fascists? Or is he more like the selfish, puritanical bigot described by Mencken? Or is he indeed the kindly man of common sense so dear to democrats like Lord Bryce? Twentieth-century political science has provided us with the methods and the data to study systematically the actual political behaviour of the average citizen.

Following the establishment of universal suffrage, statistical analyses of voting patterns began in earnest in the 1920s. In the 1930s these analyses could be supplemented by data on voting behaviour and public opinion drawn from national opinion polls, such as those of the Gallup organization. And by the mid 1950s the use of sophisticated survey-interview schedules to elicit data on the political behaviour of the average citizen had become a principal method of research employed by political scientists. All this work has uncovered a picture of the average citizen which is, as we might expect, far more complex than any of the simple descriptions suggested above.

Before describing this picture in detail, let us indicate more specifically the characteristics to be expected of these three types of citizens. Although political theorists may fail to spell out explicitly the assumptions they make regarding citizens' characteristics, they cannot avoid making such assumptions – either implicitly or explicitly – if they intend their theories to serve as plausible descriptions of how politics ought to be conducted. Table 1 summarizes our expectations of the characteristics of citizens in seven areas of citizenship as suggested by the liberal-democratic, elitist, and fascist political theories reviewed in this and preceding chapters.

For interest in politics the contrasts between the three types of citizens are quite clear. The liberal democrat is expected to maintain a constant and high interest in politics. For him the admonition: 'Eternal vigilance is the price of liberty!' represents not a tired *cliché*, but a motto to live by. In contrast elitist theorists characterize the average citizen's interest in politics as generally low. On those infrequent occasions when he does become interested, however, this citizen is expected to become rather passionately concerned. He rarely shows a constant dispassionate interest. The fascist citizen, like the liberal democrat, is supposed to maintain a high interest in politics, but in contrast to the liberal democrat who defines politics for himself, the fascist citizen accepts what his leader defines as politics. In the same polity, therefore, a liberal democrat and a fascist would be likely to disagree about what sorts of acts or issues were political.

Table 1   Expected Characteristics of Average Citizens as Suggested by Liberal Democratic, Elitist, and Fascist Political Theories

	Liberal Democrat	*Elitist*	*Fascist*
1 Interest in politics	High, constant	Inconstant, usually low; occasionally highly passionate	High, constant; but leadership defines politics
2 Knowledge of political system	High	Low	High
3 Knowledge of current issues	High, at least on issues of concern	Low	High, but limited to prescribed sources of information.
4 Concern about current issues	High to low as individual chooses	Usually low but occasionally passionately high; rarely moderate	High to low as leader directs
5 Participation in policy decisions	High turnout; constant participation on issues of concern	Usually low turnout; occasionally high participation on issues of concern	Plebiscites only as directed by leader. High response to calls for activism. Low rates of initiation of policy
6 Concern for civil rights, minority dissent	High	Low	Low
7 Consistency and coherence of attitudes and opinions	High	Low	Consistent adherence to leadership line. Line may be inconsistent or incoherent

A liberal democrat and a fascist do resemble one another on the second dimension: both are expected to know a great deal about their own political system. In reality, however, the fascist knows only what his leadership allows him to know; but the expectation is that the fascist, like the democrat will be quite knowledgeable about the formal aspects of his government. In contrast elitists expect that the average citizen will know rather little about how his government is organized and who are his public officials.

On knowledge of current issues there remains a superficial resemblance between the liberal democrat and the fascist. Both are knowledgeable in this area, but the liberal democrat tends to choose his own sources of information while the fascist citizen is limited to sources approved (and usually controlled) by his government. The elitists believe the average citizen simply knows very little about current issues.

According to the elitists one reason why the average citizen knows so little about current issues is that in general he is not concerned about them. He would rather pursue his own private interests than burden himself with the affairs of state. When some issue impinges upon his private life, however, the elitists expect the citizen often to react with passionate, though still uninformed, concern about the issue. The liberal democrat and the fascist citizen on the other hand are usually more concerned about current issues. But the liberal democrat will choose his own concerns by and large, while the fascist citizen will become concerned only with those issues towards which the leadership directs his attention.

Participation in policy decisions brings out some stark contrasts in expected characteristics. The liberal-democratic citizen is expected to exercise his franchise regularly and to take active roles in the politics surrounding issues of concern to him. These active roles include both initiation of and reaction to demands concerning resolution of the issues. The fascist citizen, though an active participant, restricts his electoral activity to choices, often presented as plebiscites, laid out by the leadership. He rarely plays a role in initiating demands for a particular resolution of a political issue. The elitists' average citizen often fails to vote. He usually avoids other forms of political participation also, but on infrequent occasions he is likely to enter the political arena with the passionate ignorance of the proverbial bull in a china shop, bent on achieving his way regardless of the damage he may inflict.

Of the three types of citizen only the liberal democrat is expected to have concern for the rights and privileges of those who disagree with him. The elitist citizen proceeds with a bigoted unconcern for the opinions of those who disagree with him. The fascist citizen is even worse. He has received the truth from his leaders, and so he knows that those who disagree with him are absolutely wrong. If they do not mend their ways, therefore, those who oppose the fascist citizen's goals may be sacrificed to those goals. In plain English, they may be exterminated.

The liberal democrat is the only one of the three types of citizens who is expected to show a consistent and coherent ideology. When the average citizen considers an issue, the elitists see him concerned only with the immediate consequences for himself. He cannot bother to consider the long-term consequences even for himself, let alone the consequences for others and the complex relationships of those consequences to the resolution of other issues. The fascists insist only upon passionate adherence to the positions advocated by the leadership. They fully admit, even boast, that such positions may be based upon emotion rather than logic. 'All great movements are popular movements, volcanic eruptions of human passions and emotional sentiments, stirred either by the cruel Goddess of Distress or by the firebrand of the word hurled among the masses; they are not the lemonade-like outpourings of the literary aesthetes and drawing-room heroes,' wrote Hitler.[5]

Which of these characterizations is most correct? Let us now examine the facts.

4

The Average Citizen in Fact. With regard to interest in politics, the elitist theorists clearly come closest to the mark. If there is one thing political scientists can tell us for certain, it is that most people have but sporadic interest in politics. Numerous studies have found that only about one third of the adult populations of the United States and Britain (and/or other Western countries as well) claim to follow politics regularly. At the same time, between one fourth and one third freely admit they have little or no interest in politics. Even at election time interest remains relatively low. Over one quarter of the electorates of Britain and the United States regularly profess little or no interest in current political campaigns.[6]

Yet, as elitist theorists contend, episodic interest in politics is not uncommon. And its most notable occurrences tend to reflect poorly upon the reputed good sense of the average citizen. Moreover the foci of political interest tend to be defined by political leaders, often in a manner conforming to fascist expectations of citizen behaviour.

Mencken himself wrote *Notes on Democracy* during a period of national 'prohibition', when an alliance of feminists, moralists, teetotalers, and industrialists, many of whom were otherwise unconcerned with party politics, had successfully pushed through a constitutional amendment banning the manufacture and sale of alcoholic beverages. Needless to say, their naïve hopes that closing the wineries, breweries, distilleries, and saloons would substantially reduce problems of poverty, crime, insanity, debauchery, degeneracy, and infidelity – not to mention 'blue Monday' industrial absenteeism – remained largely unfulfilled. Bootlegging and pious hypocrisy in politics abounded, however.

Hard on the heels of prohibition came the first great American 'red scare'. Encouraged (and often directed) by Attorney-General A. Mitchel Palmer, red-blooded American police, supported by a red-blooded American public, locked up thousands of suspected Bolsheviks on the flimsiest of evidence. May Day 1920 saw mobilization of the national guard to ward off the imminent communist overthrow of the United States government, which Palmer warned was slated for that day. So effective were Palmer's measures that May Day passed without one bomb, without even one shot fired by a red revolutionary. Although some detractors had the temerity to suggest that perhaps there were no reds ready to revolt, Palmer, like the man who shreds newspapers in the New York subway to keep away the elephants, exulted in the effectiveness of his precautionary measures. A generation later, when Palmer's antics were mostly forgotten, Senator Joseph McCarthy rekindled public interest in the red menace. As McCarthy waved his lists of card-carrying communists, once again politics began to capture the interest of large numbers of otherwise inattentive American citizens. Nor have many of today's Americans displayed much wiser judgements. The supporters of Governor George Wallace's national ambitions were largely drawn from independents – citizens normally indifferent to partisan politics – and from individuals who had little previous campaign experience.[7] It was Wallace's unique blend of demagoguery – a potpourri of racism, populism, and puritan morality – that aroused their political interest. And if Wallace's star has faded, then doubtless another's will soon shine in its place. And the new star's appeal is likely to be just as illiberal and demagogic.

But can we say that the political actions and opinions of Americans are any less consistent or sensible than those of citizens of other countries? Turning to Britain we may ask: Did those who supported J. Enoch Powell's break with the Conservative Party show any more consistent interest in politics than did those who supported Mr Wallace's rebellion against the national Democratic Party? Were their concerns any more noble? Were the anti-immigration voters who defeated Foreign Secretary Patrick Gordon Walker in 1964 and 1965 any more reasonable than the anti-communist voters who defeated 'pink lady' Helen Gahagen Douglas in her contest against Richard M. Nixon for the United States Senate in 1950? Was their subsequent political participation any less episodic? Are the contemporary appeals of the National Front any more worthy than those made by fascist parties in the past? Are supporters of the Front disgruntled party regulars, or are they mostly political novices attracted by the Front's extravagant promises to make things right again: to restore law, order and prosperity, principally by repatriating every Briton who is not of Anglo-Saxon stock?

Political scientists suggest a general pattern underlies these instances of sporadic interest. Generally speaking, those with low interest in politics are more difficult to arouse to action about any issue than are ordinary citizens. But when their interest is aroused, they tend to become more active and more passionately involved than ordinary citizens. This passionate involvement stems from the fact that unlike ordinary citizens, low-interest citizens have fewer traditional political loyalties, less knowledge of reasons for opposition to their positions, and less knowledge of the ordinary processes and channels for political expression. When significant portions of the approximately one-in-four citizens with low interest become interested in the same matter, their impact tends to be stronger than we might expect simply from their number, for they proceed to enter into political activity with a passion that exceeds that of ordinary citizens.[8] Thus the sudden rise of support for political demagogues like Senator Joseph McCarthy, Governor George Wallace, or the Right Honourable J. Enoch Powell; or of political phenomena like the Poujadist movement in France, the Dixiecrats in the United States, the National Front in the United Kingdom, or the Nazi Party in Germany. Many political scientists argue that like a little learning, a little interest in politics is often a dangerous thing. (We shall have more to say about this argument in chapter 5.)

Knowledge of the political system for the average citizen is low to moderate. Most citizens have only rudimentary (and often incorrect) knowledge about their polity's institutions. They tend to know more about national political institutions than about local ones, and they tend to have more familiarity with the names of national political leaders than with those of local leaders, but the overall level of knowledge of government is far from impressive.

In 1970 the (Kilbrandon) Commission of the Constitution found that only one Briton in three could correctly associate such basic services as primary schools, hospitals, electricity, and the postal service with the levels of government (city or county, regional, national, or independent corporation) most responsible. One in four on the other hand could associate only one or none of the services with the responsible level of government.[9] Although some studies have found that as many as 90 per cent of the electorate could name their MP at election time, this figure drops to around 50 per cent between elections. Moreover, only between one half and two thirds of the electors report having read or heard anything about their MP at election time; only one in three between elections.[10] At the local level recognition of government officials is even lower: in the mid 1960s, for example, only one of five Glaswegians could name any of the three city councillors for their ward.[11] To make matters worse, Britons show a considerable lack of ability to relate parties and political leaders. Just before the 1959 general election, Mark Abrams asked a sample of electors to name three leaders of the Conservative Party, three leaders of the Labour Party, and one leader of the Liberals. One in five could name none. Another 11 per cent could name only the Prime Minister. Only 30 per cent could produce five or more names.[12]

Americans are no more knowledgeable about their own political institutions than are Britons. At various times public opinion surveys have found that fewer than 20 per cent could correctly identify the Bill of Rights, only half knew their state had two senators, and barely two thirds knew the President's tenure was limited to two terms. About half the electorate could name their representative in Congress, and fewer than half reported having heard or read anything about him, even at election time. Only one third could name both of the senators from their state and fewer still could name their representatives or senators in the state legislature.[13]

With respect to knowledge of the political system, then, the elitist expectations about the average citizen once again come closest to the mark. With respect to knowledge of and concern about current issues, however, the situation is more complex.

When it comes to giving opinions on a wide variety of subjects, the average citizen is usually ready to oblige. Time and again pollsters have found that for most issues more than eight out of ten citizens willingly render an opinion. For issues that relate to citizens' personal experiences or that receive prominent coverage in the news media prior to the polling, the proportion is considerably higher. On more remote issues, even those which may be of major importance, the proportion having an opinion tends to be considerably lower.

Typical of this pattern in Britain are opinions about further nationalization, about the power of big business, and about the power of the unions. Over the period from 1963 to 1966 Butler and Stokes found that between 82 and 89 per cent of those interviewed rendered opinions on these subjects. In the same period, between 95 and 99 per cent of those asked gave opinions on the importance of the Royal Family and on the desired extent of immigration. For the more complex issue of the entry of the United Kingdom into the European Common Market, as late as spring of 1966, 29 per cent still admitted they held no opinion.[14]

Similar examples can be cited for the United States. In 1965 Gallup found that 83 per cent expressed opinions concerning the power of big business and that 87 per cent expressed opinions about the power of trade unions.[15] Typically, Gallup has also found that between 80 and 90 per cent of those sampled render opinions on the way the President is handling his job. On personal issues, or highly dramatic ones, such as some aspects of the war in Vietnam in the 1970s, or control of use of petrol, oil and electricity during the energy crisis of winter 1973 to 1974, the proportion with opinions has often reached 95 per cent.[16] When the issue seemed more remote, as did the war in Vietnam in 1964 (just before the massive troop and weapons escalation), as many as 39 per cent could express no opinion.[17]

Were citizens' abilities to express an opinion about an issue equivalent to their possession of knowledge about the issue, then the liberal-democrat characterization would be essentially correct. Unfortunately this is not the case. We find instead considerable evidence that citizens often render opinions without benefit of knowledge about the relevant issues.

To begin with, the situation in which citizens are asked their opinions is apt to be somewhat artificial. A friendly pollster appears, usually without prior warning, and begins to ask a series of questions about events and issues which may or may not be of real interest to those being polled. Confronted by this smiling well-groomed inquisitor, who really seems interested in their opinions, most citizens feel flattered; and some feel obliged to offer opinions even upon subjects in which they have only the remotest interest. It would be impolite, perhaps even unseemly, to disappoint or offend this inquisitive visitor by replying 'don't know' or 'no opinion' to his questions. Besides, in a democracy good citizens are *supposed* to have opinions about current issues. To appear unable to render an opinion would reflect poorly upon the performance of their roles as good citizens.

Given these circumstances, studies show that large numbers of citizens are perfectly willing to give definite opinions upon subjects of which they know nothing and care little. Examples of such behaviour are easy to find. In 1961, for instance, Gallup found 68 per cent of the British public ready to render an opinion about the effects of Britain's joining the Common Market, yet only 31 per cent understood that Britain was already a member of the European Free Trade Area, but not of the Common Market.[18] Some 91 per cent of the approximately one third of all citizens whom the Kilbrandon Commission rated as having little or no knowledge of which government bodies controlled various government services, nonetheless volunteered ratings on the current performance of the 'present system of governing Britain'. Even among the one in five citizens whom interviewers rated as having great difficulty in understanding the questionnaire, some 85 per cent readily rendered opinions on overall governmental performance.[19] A national survey of Americans in 1956 found that across sixteen selected campaign issues, 65 per cent of the electorate on average held an opinion and knew what the government was doing. Nonetheless, another 20 per cent on average expressed an opinion, even though they had no idea what Government policy was regarding the issue.[20] In 1965 Gallup found that notwithstanding that only 19 per cent knew how their congressman voted on any major bill and only 14 per cent knew of anything he had done for the district, 53 per cent of the American public were willing, nevertheless, to rate the congressman's performance of his job – A, B, C, D, or Flunk! [21]

To complicate matters further, the way questions are worded may encourage particular response patterns. To cite some well-known examples, studies of the 'authoritarian personality' conducted in the late 1940s found that less-educated working-class individuals appeared more authoritarian than did their more educated middle-class brethren. Subsequent studies revealed that this working-class 'authoritarianism' resulted largely from the fact that an affirmative answer was scored as authoritarian. As it happened, working-class respondents were more likely to express agreement to middle-class interviewers than were middle-class respondents. [22] Similarly, studies of opinion of the war in Vietnam usually found 'hawkish' majorities when phrases like 'communist takeover', 'American defeat', or 'loss of American credibility' were evoked, but 'dovish' majorities when the phrases used were 'domestic costs', 'killings', or 'continuing the war'.[23]

If the preponderance of public opinion thus stems from the turn of a phrase, it follows that the concern citizens have for most political issues must be rather slight. Indeed numerous studies have indicated that compared to personal problems – maintaining one's health, finding good work, making ends meet, raising a family – political problems come a distant second.[24] Even on political problems like nationalization in Britain or control of big business in the United States, which have been debated publicly for more than a generation, studies suggest that no more than half the respective electorates have developed any deeply held convictions.[25]

Yet it would be unfair to conclude that the elitist description of a citizenry with low interest and low concern about political issues is entirely correct. Our conclusion depends upon our perspective. If we take the pollsters' issues, then we find that opinions may be common, but knowledge and concern are mostly moderate or low. If we view political issues from the citizens' perspectives, we come to a different conclusion.

Citizens are knowledgeable and concerned about *some* political issues, but their concerns tend to be somewhat idiosyncratic, *i.e.*, those issues which interest citizen A do not necessarily (or even usually) interest citizen B. Nonetheless, on political issues which excite their interest, citizens' behaviours tend to fulfil the liberal democrats' expectations. A study by David RePass serves to illustrate this point: RePass found that among a national sample of Americans in 1964, over 80 per cent listed at least one political problem as 'on their mind a lot' or 'causing extreme worry'. Towards each issue named in this manner over 60 per cent on

85

average saw differences in the Democratic and Republican Party positions. This despite the fact that no single issue was named by more than 12 per cent of sample.[26]

Our conclusions concerning the appropriateness of the liberal-democratic and elitist characterizations of citizens' knowledge and concern about issues, therefore, must remain uncertain. Although both characterizations fit the facts better than does the fascist view, neither is entirely satisfactory. True, as elitists contend, for almost any given political issue, a majority of citizens have little knowledge or concern. But also true, as liberal democrats contend, a large majority of citizens have considerable knowledge and concern about selected political issues they consider to be of personal importance.

For participation in policy decisions, our conclusions are similarly uncertain. Most citizens by no means participate in the day-to-day decision making of government, but they do exercise their franchise, and they are willing to take specific steps to make their opinions known to responsible officials on important issues of personal interest. Table 2 summarizes the frequency with which citizens in Britain and the United States report participation in various common types of political activity.

At first blush it might appear as if the average citizen engaged in a minimal number of political activities. As shown, paying attention to and voting in national elections are the only activities in which a majority report participation. This might suggest that citizens' influence over public-policy decisions, regardless of their personal importance, was largely limited to expressing policy preferences through their votes – a method of expression of dubious validity, as we shall see.

This suggested interpretation would be inaccurate. Studies show that the activities listed are not necessarily of a cumulative nature. That is, those who participate in less common activities do not necessarily participate in more common ones. Many people, for instance, who contact local officials about issues of personal concern, nonetheless fail to vote, especially in local elections. Similarly, significant portions of nominal party members – and even some party subscribers or contributors – also fail to vote.[27] In fact when all the listed activities are considered, it

Table 2   Participation in Political Activity*
(Percentages)

United States	%	*United Kingdom*	%
1 Follow Presidential campaign on television (1964)	89	1 Follow General Elections in Media or Personal Conversation (1964)	92
2 Pay much or a little attention to Political Campaigns (1960)	87	2 Pay much or a little attention to political campaigns (1959)	71
3 Report voting regularly in presidential elections (1967)	72	3 Report voting in 1964 General Election (1970)	77 (72)
4 Report always voting in local elections (1967)	47	4 Report voting in local elections where contested (1964)	43
5 Active in at least one organization involved in community affairs (1967)	32	5 Nominal members of political party (including trade-union membership) (1964)	25
6 Member of organization active in political affairs (1960)	24	6 Member of organization active in political affairs (1959)	19
7 Ever contacted local government official about some issue or problem at least once (1967)	20	7 Ever contacted a (local) local official or (county) county office (1970)	18 26
8 Ever contacted state or national official about some issue or problem at least once (1967)	18	8 Ever contacted MP about any issue or problem at least once (1970)	8
9 (not available)		9 Ever complained to public or private corporation (at least 26% to public corporations)	40
10 Ever formed a group to attempt to solve community problem	14	10 (not available)	
11 Ever given money to candidate or party (1967)	13	11 Subscribed to local party (1964)	14

Table 2 (*cont.*)   Participation in Political Activity*

United States	%	United Kingdom	%
12 Attended a meeting during election campaign (1952–68)	Varies 7–14	12 Attended political campaign meeting during 1964 general election	8
13 Worked actively for a political candidate (1952–68)	3–5†	13 'Political Attitude' (1972)	7‡
14 Held public or party office	less than 1	14 Held public or party office (1964)	less than 1

*SOURCES: Butler and Stokes, p. 25; Commission on Constitution, pp. 24–6; Verba and Nie (see note 28) p. 31; Almond and Verba, p. 89; Flanigan, p. 106; Rose (see note 44) p. 192; *Codebook: SRC-CPS 1964 Presidential Election Study*, Ann Arbor, Michigan, Inter-University Consortium for Political Research.

†26 per cent report having worked for a party or candidate in at least one election.

‡Citizens engaged in at least 5 of the above types of activities. See Rose p. 190.

turns out that approximately one half of the electors in Britain and the United States engage in one or more of the activities listed in the table which are less common than voting or mere nominal membership in a community or party organization.[28] Furthermore, studies suggest that a majority of citizens would participate more fully if they felt strongly enough about a given issue, and that they would expect to succeed in their attempts to rectify an unjust local or national regulation.[29] Finally, those who engage in these activities generally show a sophisticated appreciation of the appropriate ways to achieve their aims. The authors of *Participation in America*, the most comprehensive study available on current political activity, conclude:

Our data on the content of citizen initiated contacts show a citizenry involved with the government in ways that are highly salient to them, on issues that they define, and through channels that seem appropriate. What we are suggesting is that on matters of the politics of everyday life, citizens know what they want.[30]

The elitist characterization is correct once again, but only insofar as we find that for nearly every given political activity which might influence public policy, a majority of citizens fail to participate. And the liberal-democratic characterization is also correct; but only to the extent that about half the citizens do engage in *some* potentially influential political activity, other than merely voting or belonging to a community organization. Only the fascist characterization is entirely off the mark.

Despite the periodic bursts of articles in the popular press, deploring the intolerance of diversity and the pressures towards conformity found in modern society, systematic studies of citizens' concerns for the rights of others are less than conclusive about the supposed prevalence of intolerance and conformity. On the one hand citizens show a rather firm commitment to liberal-democratic principles, such as equal treatment before the law, opportunity to express dissent, freedom to organize and pool political resources, and the right to conduct free and open election of leaders. On the other hand citizens show considerably less commitment to specific applications of these principles. In much the way that elitist and fascist theorists predict, they express intolerance of protesters, non-conformists, communists, and others who espouse minority causes.

A well-known study by James Prothro and Charles Grigg, for instance, found over 90 per cent of American electors in two cities in the late 1950s favoured statements like 'Every citizen should have an equal chance to influence government policy,' 'The minority should be free to criticize majority decisions,' and 'People in the minority should be free to try to win majority support for their opinions.' But when the same electors were asked about what were apparently specific instances of these statements – whether only rate-payers should be allowed to vote in local tax referenda (no); whether a communist should be allowed to make a public speech in favour of communism (yes); whether the American Medical Association had a right to increase its (minority) influence by urging members to vote as a bloc (yes) – majorities opted for the anti-democratic responses of yes, no and no.[31] A replication of this study conducted in London in 1962 found a similar pattern of results, except that majorities usually favoured the liberal-democratic responses to the specific statements though by considerably smaller percentages than they favoured them for the corresponding general statement.[32] Moreover, to the delight of elitist theorists, the London study also corroborated an American finding that professional politicians and party leaders were more likely to support liberal-democratic alternatives than were members of the general public.[33]

Subsequent studies have served to muddy the waters. In the mid 1960s in Glasgow no consistent differences were found between city councillors and electors regarding endorsements of majority against minority decisions on current issues. To the extent that patterns appeared, both groups tended to support majority or minority stands in accordance with their own or their party's stand on the issue.[34] A comparative study of the attitudes towards democratic procedures of electors and councillors in Belfast and Glasgow found no consistent differences regarding support of democratic procedures, despite the obvious differences in actual manner in which politics are conducted in the two cities.[35] Nor did the recent conduct of Mr Nixon and all his men provide much support for elitist contentions that public leaders have a far higher regard for democratic principles and procedures than do the ordinary citizens.

It is true that citizens support general principles of democracy to a greater extent than they do specific applications of those principles. They support civil rights, but deplore demonstrations – even legal ones – to secure those rights.[36] They support racial equality, but they deplore many of the practical means of achieving it;[37] they believe in free speech, but would censor certain persons or ideas. [38] But it is also true that no conclusive proof has been presented that the so-called elite – professional politicians, captains of industry, gentlemen, or soldiers – have any greater respect for or allegiance to democratic norms. Moreover, whenever such elites apparently show greater support for such norms, this support can usually be shown as a function of the elites' greater average level of education or greater level of exposure to political phenomena. But both these characteristics are precisely those which many democratic theorists, must notably

John Stuart Mill, have long urged as fundamental requisites for a responsible democratic citizenry.[39] Liberal democrats rightly point out that these findings are entirely consistent with their pleas for government to provide for greater educational and participatory opportunities for the average citizen.

On the last listed characteristic, consistency and coherence of attitudes and opinions, the elitist characterization once more corresponds most closely to reality. By even the most generous estimates, less than one quarter of the British or American electorates can be said to have a coherent ideology. Most citizens judge political issues on the basis of their immediately perceived impact, paying little attention either to long-term consequences or to the relation of one issue to another. Nor do a majority view the political parties, the vehicles for organizing issues into coherent programmes, as arrayed along a left-right or liberal-conservative continuum.[40]

Even though the average American will classify himself – at the pollster's behest – as liberal, conservative, or middle of the road, these labels do not correspond to patterns of opinion the elector actually holds. In their well-known study *The Political Beliefs of Americans* Free and Cantril found that 44 per cent of those who classified themselves as conservatives held opinions on federal aid to education, federal aid to housing, Medicare, urban renewal, and the Poverty Program, which could be classified only as liberal.[41] Other studies have shown that ideology has at least two dimensions, domestic and foreign, and that liberalism or conservativism with regard to domestic issues does not correspond with liberalism or conservatism with regard to foreign affairs.[42]

On the British side class identification is sometimes thought to serve as a substitute for ideology. There are strong correspondences between working-class identification and support for the Labour party; also between middle-class identification and support for the Conservative Party.[43] But neither class nor party identification has been found relevant for determining British electors' stands on issues like capital punishment for criminals, corporal punishment for schoolboys, immigration policy, farm subsidies, cuts in government spending, control of political demonstrations, and (before 1970) entry into the Common Market.[44]

All this does not mean that ideology or its approximates, class and party identification, are irrelevant to electors' policy preferences. There are many issues – in Britain, expanded nationalization, comprehensive schools and relating state pensions to earnings; and, in America, fair-employment practices, Medicare and guarantee of a minimum standard of living – upon which the opinions held by working-class identifiers, Labourites and Democrats are opposed to those held by their counterparts.[45] Indeed recent studies suggest that as educational levels have increased over the past two decades, so too have the proportions of electors who view political issues from an ideological standpoint. The burgeoning numbers of such electors – though they remain a distinct minority – have led some theorists to predict a resurgence of ideological politics as those under thirty mature and move into positions of greater political influence.[46] If these theorists are correct, the liberal-democratic characterization may yet emerge as more accurate than the elitists' in the foreseeable future.

5

Conclusions. Our examination of the characteristics of the average citizen produces some discouraging results for liberal democrats. Although the liberal-democratic characterization of the citizen is more accurate than the fascist characterization, the elitist characterization seems the most accurate of the three. Referring back to Table 1, the elitist characterization seems to fit the facts better than does the liberal-democratic on characteristics 1, 2 and 7, and no worse than does the liberal-democratic on characteristics 3 to 6. What implications do these findings have regarding the viability of liberal democracy?

On the one hand a theory of liberal democracy, as should any theory which purports to describe an attainable state of affairs, must correspond to the facts. In this case it should require arrangements of citizen duties and political institutions which come within the capabilities of average citizens to fulfil. If it makes demands which require more governmental capacities from ordinary citizens than we can reasonably expect them to possess, then the theory is not a realistic one, and the democracy it describes is not viable. We would not ignore such a theory, but we would relegate it to the nether reaches reserved for pure utopias – pictures of societies and governments which we might strive for, but cannot realistically expect to attain.[47]

On the other hand a theory of liberal democracy, as should any theory which purports to incorporate certain values, must describe a state of affairs in which those values are preserved. In this case the key values desired are not only those of democracy alone – i.e., those which prize equal opportunity for participation in politics – but also the liberal values which prize citizen participation in the determination of social goals and the maximization of opportunity for individual self-expression and development. If the theory describes a state of affairs which largely precludes the attainment of these latter values, then it no longer deserves the word *liberal* in its title, regardless of how democratic it might be.[48]

We face a dilemma. It may not be possible to develop a theory of liberal democracy which is compatible with both the empirically demonstrated capabilities of the citizenry and the theoretically demonstrated necessity of preserving liberal values. If we choose an alternative one – shaping the theory the better to fit reality – we may be forced to abandon some key values essential to liberalism. If we choose alternative two – shaping the theory the better to accommodate liberal values – we may produce nothing more than a Utopian vision.

As political scientists in Britain and the United States have developed better empirical data bases, their confidence in the accuracy of their observations of the political behaviour of the average citizen has grown. As a result there has been growing pressure to choose the first alternative, to shape the theory of liberal democracy to fit the facts as observed. In recent years three major types of revised theories of democracy have emerged, each laying emphasis upon certain features of modern society which are said to make up for the citizens' failures to display the behavioural characteristics liberal democrats have described.

93

The first type lays emphasis upon the multiplicity of interest groups that exist in modern society; the second takes note of the pervasiveness and importance of the political parties; and the third emphasizes the importance of political socialization and the recruitment of properly trained leaders. But all of them have one feature in common: they lean more heavily upon elitist characterizations of individual citizens than they do upon liberal-democratic ones.

To these revised theories of democracy, and to the critiques of these theories, we now turn our attention.

5 · Revised Theories of Democracy

However, if there is anything to be said for the processes that actually distinguish democracy (or polyarchy) from dictatorship, it is not discoverable in the clear-cut distinction between government by a majority and government by a minority. The distinction comes much closer to being one between government by a minority and government by *minorities*.
Robert A. Dahl, *A Preface to Democratic Theory*, University of Chicago Press, 1956.

Democracy is a competitive political system in which competing leaders and organizations define alternatives of public policy in such a way that the public can participate in the decision-making process. . . . Democracy is not to be found *in* the parties but *between* the parties.
E. E. Schattschneider, *The Semi-Sovereign People*, Holt, Rinehart & Winston, 1960 and *Party Government*, Holt, Rinehart & Winston, 1942.

. . . the political influentials manifest by comparison with ordinary voters a more developed sense of ideology and a firmer grasp of its [American Democracy's] essentials. This is evidenced by their stronger approval of democratic ideas, their greater tolerance and regard for proper procedures and citizen rights, their superior understanding and acceptance of 'rules of the game,' and their more affirmative attitudes toward the political system in general.
Herbert McClosky 'Consensus and Ideology in American Politics', *American Political Science Review*, LVIII, 1964.

Then let's rejoice with loud Fal la-Fal lal la!
That nature always does contrive-Fal lal la!
That every boy and every gal
   That's born into the world alive

Viable Democracy
Is either a little Liberal
  Or else a little Conservative!
W. S. Gilbert, *Iolanthe*, 1882.

I

If, as political scientists tell us, the average citizen seldom behaves as Good Citizen Brown; if he concerns himself mainly with family and financial affairs instead of with politics; if he considers the few political problems, which happen to come to his attention without regard to their relationship to one another or to an overall ideology; if he rarely initiates policy and often fails even to vote; then how are we to salvage a theory of liberal democracy for the last decades of the twentieth century?

One solution is to modify the concept of liberal democracy to accommodate elitist interpretations of the findings of modern empirical research. The theories presented in the next three portions of this chapter dismiss the idea that democracy requires the presence of an informed, rationally self-interested citizenry. Instead they assign the job of maintaining democracy to interest groups, political parties, or those social institutions responsible for the socialization of political leaders.

As these theories are ostensibly induced from scientific observations of citizens' political behaviour, they have gained widespread acceptance within the discipline of political science since the Second World War. Moreover, these theories have seemed so persuasive that only since the mid sixties have most political scientists begun to take seriously some longstanding criticisms of their emasculated concept of democracy, much less to consider the possible consequences of adopting such a concept.

The recent resurgence of critiques of these revised theories of democracy will be examined in the later portions of this chapter.

2

Group Theory. Although discussions of the roles of differing interests in the political system can be found as far back in time as Ancient Greece and Rome in the works of Aristotle and Polybius, the theory that politics – and hence democratic politics – consists of the struggles among groups, not individuals, seeking to manipulate the environment to their own advantage received its twentieth-century impetus from the work of Arthur Bentley (1870–1957). In 1908 Bentley published his landmark study, *The Process of Government.*[1]

Bentley describes his work as 'an attempt to fashion a tool' for political analysis. He did not believe that the utilitarian conception of the individual citizen rationally calculating the pleasure or pain of each political act explained very much. For that matter he did not believe that any set of values or ideas provided adequate explanations of political behaviour. From where did the individual derive his values? From where did he get his motivations and desires? His ideas and feelings, Bentley answered, reflected his social activity. They arose from his interactions with others, interactions which took place within group contexts. Ideas, values, motivations and the like were dependent variables, the origins of which could be found in the patterns of social interaction among groups. Meaningful explanation of political behaviour would be found by studying the activity of groups in the political arena, not by studying the ideas or motivations of individuals.

And how does one study activity? Not at random but in the most exacting and scientific manner possible. Systematic observation and measurement were the keys to the development of a viable quantitative political science:

> If a statement of social facts which lends itself better to measurement is offered, that characteristic entitles it to attention. Providing the statement does not otherwise distort the social facts, the capability of measurement will be decisive in its favor. The statement that takes us farthest along the road toward quantitative estimates will inevitably be the best statement.[2]

Bentley followed his preliminary arguments with a lengthy analysis of the actual process of government in which he attempted to apply his precepts. And even though this analysis failed to satisfy Bentley's own admonitions regarding quantification – he was, after all, only attempting to fashion a tool – it nonetheless contained an insightful interpretation of the American political process, an interpretation destined to have a profound influence on the twentieth-century political science.

For Bentley politics consisted of the struggle among interest groups to gain power to promote said interests and to achieve the groups' goals. Each group acted in its own interest, not for some higher value, such as the greatest good for the greatest number. The job of government in the broadest sense was the adjustment and accommodation of group interests. Groups acted upon governmental institution at all phases of policy-making: at elections, in the legislature, in the executive and bureaucracy, even in the judiciary. In the last analysis law consisted of nothing more than the habitual activities of dominant interest groups. These groups had successfully persuaded government to enforce conformity to the patterns of behaviour they desired.

Throughout his political analysis Bentley avoided moral judgements regarding the propriety of the group struggle or its results. He was bent on developing a scientific method for studying politics, not upon evaluating the political process or its outcomes from any moral standpoint. Indeed, such an exercise would have caused him great difficulty, for he had spent a good deal of time arguing that ideas and values were themselves only reflections of group activity.

The Process of Government, now considered a classic statement of twentieth-century empirical political science, was slow in being recognized as such. Notwithstanding generally favourable reviews in several scholarly journals, for nearly thirty years political scientists largely ignored the book. Only in the 1930s, when the behavioural school of political science first emerged, was Bentley's work 'rediscovered'.[3] In 1935 a second edition was published. Still it was not until the 1950s that Bentley's influence and importance became widely acknowledged. By then behavioural political science had at last become a major interest of students of American government. Betokening this acknowledgement were the publication of David Truman's *The Governmental Process* (1951) and Bertram Gross's *The Legislative Struggle* (1953), both of which drew their analytic framework (and, in the former case, its title) directly from *The Process of Government*.[4]

For our purposes the important point is not so much that these newer works established Bentley's conception of politics – the struggle for power among interest groups – as a central analytical tool for political scientists, but that they raised competition among groups to a normative principle of government. Where Bentley had only suggested that theorists judge the extent of democracy in a polity by examining the balance of power among groups struggling for control of government, Truman and Gross proceeded to identify democracy with a pluralistic struggle among diversified interest groups. They further judged that the distribution of power among interest groups in the United States was indeed democratic – that no small set of the multifarious interest groups controlled disproportionate numbers of political policy decisions.[5]

The equation of modern democracy with pluralistic competition among groups gained widespread acceptance among the emerging generation of political scientists. This post-war generation had become increasingly aware of empirical evidence of the type reviewed in the last chapter, which indicated that Americans (and others) failed to live up to Jeffersonian standards of rationality. If the survival of democracy depended upon the modern equivalent of the sturdy yeomanry – resourceful citizens exercising independent political judgement about the issues of the day – then democracy would soon be extinct. But if the burden of support for democracy were shifted from the individual citizen to organized interest groups, the prospects for its survival would look brighter.

The virtues of groups would make up for the failures of the individual citizen. Was the citizen ignorant of many political issues which affected his interests? The groups which looked out for his interests would protect him. Did the ordinary citizen lack the means to make his wishes known to his representatives or to the public at large? The groups would pool the modest resources of ordinary citizens, aggregate their interests, and articulate them to the relevant decision-making bodies. Was the citizen intolerant of opposition, ready to disregard the rights of those with whom he disagreed? The interest groups favouring his cause would moderate his demands and protect the rights of others by seeking accommodation with those groups which formed the opposition.

By acting to check one another's power; by channelling citizen demands to political officials; by protecting their members' rights against encroachments of overzealous officials, demagogues, or aspiring dictators; interest groups actualize democracy. As typified by the quotation from Robert Dahl heading this chapter, group theories contend that democracy is the free interaction of diverse minorities. In a democracy there is a struggle for power among a multiplicity of interest groups in which no single interest, majority or minority, emerges as a clear-cut winner on all issues of concern. That means an interest group that dominates one area of policy will fail to dominate other areas. *Minorities* – plural – will rule.[6]

The ready acceptance of this group theory of democracy by American political scientists, however, cannot be attributed solely to its compatibility with the findings of empirical research into public opinion and voting behaviour. The emphasis of group theory on the importance of the procedures and processes of politics rather than the values inherent in the outcomes of those processes is compatible with the tenets of Social Darwinism, which, as indicated previously, have retained popularity among Americans. Under the assumption that competition among groups is relatively open, group theorists need not worry about questions of fairness and equity of the outcomes. Those groups which emerge triumphant are by definition the fittest; their very success indicates their superiority.

That no group dominates in all important issue areas seems a sufficient condition to guarantee democracy for most group theorists.[7] They presume that this condition of incomplete domination results from essentially equal opportunity for participation. Also, they tend to look askance at an overly participative citizenry, preferring instead the stable channels of communication between citizens and political officials provided by established groups. Normal politics, as seen by group theorists, consists of the resolution of conflict among groups. Citizens ought not to participate directly in policy formulation, except to vote. Indeed studies of public opinion and voting behaviour show that most citizens do not possess the competence to govern directly. They should participate indirectly through membership in interest groups or through identification with groups which support their interests and values.

But what, other than their vaunted diversity, prevents the most influential groups from combining their strengths to exploit the masses? The group theorists suggest that groups' actions are limited first by the democratic values to which group leaders have been socialized and secondly by the presence of political resources available to citizens who wish to dissent. Should established groups violate the broad general consensus regarding democratic values, potential interest groups stand ready to enter the fray to defend those values. And, mobilizing the previously unused resources, group theorists expect that these new groups could be very effective indeed.

For example, when President Nixon nominated Clement Haynesworth and Harold Carswell as Justices of the Supreme Court in 1969 and 1970, there arose such enormous opposition that the Senate took the unprecedented step of turning down both nominations. Yet prior to his nomination, most Americans had heard of neither man. The fact that the nominees did not conform to the high standards of fairness, honesty, and integrity expected of a Supreme Court Justice caused previously unconcerned citizens to mobilize in opposition to the nominations. The potential interest groups, previously satisfied with the qualifications of Mr Nixon's Supreme Court nominees, caused rejection of Mr Nixon's new choices when they perceived that they failed to satisfy the high standards required.

Group theory made its greatest impact upon American political science, but it also affected British political science, albeit more as an analytical tool than as a normative theory of democracy. Viewing politics as a struggle among interest groups erased naïve notions that Parliament was a pillar of responsibility compared to Congress, in that it had disciplined political parties which insulated its members from the pressures of selfish interests. Studies like those of Samuel Beer, Samuel Finer, and Allen Potter soon established that group pressures were indeed present in the formulation of Parliamentary legislation; only the techniques of access to important decision-makers drew less public attention.[8] In comparison with the United States far more legislation was formulated in the bureaucracy and passed through Parliament with little amendment, when presented as new government programmes, or even without debate, when presented as statutory instruments. Consequently interest groups normally concentrated their efforts upon influencing the bureaucrats more than the legislators, often through participation in the myriad of official advisory committees to Whitehall agencies. The gentlemanly manner in which British groups operated usually rendered their presence inconspicuous, but it was highly effective in achieving desired policy:

> Viewed from Whitehall, the most powerful forces confronting (not to say arrayed against) a Government in this time were the organized bodies of producers representing the main sectors of the economy: trade unions, trade associations, and professional organizations. Pressure groups were nothing new in British politics, but in the twentieth century they had assumed a distinctively new form. In their social base, structure, purpose, political tactics, relations with Government, and the foundations of their political power, they greatly differed from the transient, voluntary associations of like-minded reformers that sought to win Victorian Parliaments over to their schemes or legislation . . .
> . . . The most obvious instrumentality which producers command and which government needs is advice . . .
> . . . a vast, untidy system of functional representation . . . has grown up alongside the older system of parliamentary representation. It is mainly through this system that the powers of advice, acquiescence, and approval are brought to bear on public policy.[9]

In contrast to their American colleagues British political scientists did not regard government by interest groups as an unqualified boon. Finer feared that anonymity of policy-making within the bureaucracy coupled with the emptiness of Parliamentary debates over policy afforded easy opportunity for powerful interests to trade off favours with one another at the expense of the unorganized general public. Even Bernard Crick, who, like Bentley, asserted that politics was nothing more than the conciliation of differing interests, went to some length to differentiate this conception of politics from that of democracy. Democracy is a political principle implying mass participation in politics; politics itself can consist of competition among groups of elites.[10]

3

Party Democracy. Pioneer though he was, Bentley did not stand alone in his desire to develop a scientific study of politics. Complementary to his effort, Graham Wallas (1858–1932) published *Human Nature in Politics* in 1908, the same year *The Process of Government* appeared.[11] Where Bentley emphasized the sociological influence of the group upon the individual, Wallas focused on the psychology of the individual and its consequences for the democratic governance of the polity. Unlike Bentley, Wallas was willing to consider individuals' thoughts and feelings – human nature, if you will – as an independent variable. But like Bentley, he did not believe that the utilitarian conception of the rational citizen was accurate. This 'intellectualist assumption' led to false expectations of citizen behaviour, and these led to unrealistic theories of democratic government.

The unfortunate truth, as Wallas saw it, was that political behaviour was largely irrational, based upon instinct and emotion, not reason. As an elected official on both the London School Board and London County Council, Wallas spoke from experience on this matter. He saw first hand that as exercises in the rational selection of policy or leadership, elections failed miserably:

At my last contest for the London County Council I had to spend half an hour before the close of the vote in one of the polling stations ... The voters who came in were the results of the 'final rally' of the canvassers on both sides. They entered the room in rapid but irregular succession, as if they were jerked forward by a hurried and inefficient machine ... All were dazed and bewildered ... Most of them seemed to be trying, in the unfamiliar surroundings, to be sure of the name for which, as they had been reminded at the door, they were to vote. A few were drunk ... I was very anxious to win ..., but my chief feeling was intense conviction that this could not be accepted as even a decently satisfactory method of creating a government for a city of five million inhabitants ... [12]

Noting the failure of citizens' behaviour to conform to the liberal-democratic expectations, was only the first step towards a scientific, empirically accurate theory of democracy. Wallas sought nothing less than to:

estimate, with no desire except to arrive at truth, both the degree to which the political strengh of the individual citizen can, in any given time, be actually increased by moral or educational changes, and the possibility of preserving or extending or inventing such elements in the structure of democracy as may prevent the demand upon him being too great for his strength. [13]

That the aims of this book are so similar to those Wallas described, attests to both the relevance and the difficulty of accomplishing his task.

If Wallas, like Bentley, was more successful in making a case for a science of politics than in demonstrating its development, it does not diminish the intellectual importance of his work. Prior to the appearance of *Human Nature in Politics*, political science in the universities was largely based on moral philosophy. Its theory consisted of comment and criticisms of the worthiness of the visions of the polity presented by great thinkers like Hobbes, Locke, and Rousseau. After the appearance of Wallas's book, political science became more behavioural, studying the empirical appropriateness of such visions as well as their moral worth.

Ironically Wallas, an Englishman, had more immediate influence on American political scientists than he did on his British colleagues. Where Britain had but a handful of universities, dominated by the orthodoxy of the Oxbridge nexus, America had a multiplicity, which, for good and for ill, were less bound by scholarly tradition. In 1910 A. Lawrence Lowell brought Wallas to Harvard to lecture and lead a seminar on psychology and politics. Here he impressed not only faculty members like Lowell and Arthur Holcombe, both of whom later served as presidents of the American Political Science Association, but also the brilliant Walter Lippmann, then an undergraduate. Lippmann's *Preface to Politics* (1912) would soon popularize Wallas's ideas.

Wallas also established contact with Charles E. Merriam at the University of Chicago, and with Herbert Croly, one of the founders of the New School for Social Research. Indeed he returned to America in 1919 to lecture during the New School's inaugural year. That same year he also gave lectures at Yale, Harvard and Chicago.[14]

For our present purposes the most important aspect of *Human Nature in Politics* is not its scientific thrust, but Wallas's view of the political parties. To his mind the political party represented the most effective modern adjustment of political institutions to the realities of human nature. Wisely, the party did not rely upon the intellectual capacities of the citizenry to distinguish its candidates and programmes. Instead it attempted to build a popular image in the public mind by employing easily identifiable symbols and slogans. Wallas recognized mass political advertising for all its vileness as the wave of the future, the appropriate strategic response to the fact that most voters chose their political leaders out of habit and affection, much the way they chose their brand of tea.

All this did not disturb Wallas as much as it might an old-fashioned liberal democrat with all his unfounded 'intellectualist' assumptions about the rational nature of human behaviour. Even though most of his supporters might choose him out of habit and affection for his party, a sincere political leader could nonetheless use his position to lead his party and his government towards policies which tended to benefit all members of the polity, not some narrow section of it. Wallas cited Sir Robert Peel's reversal of party policy in 1845 from restrictive trade to repeal of the Corn Laws as an admirable, although not entirely successful example of such progressive leadership. As a founder of the Fabian Society, Wallas himself had hoped to encourage such leadership within the socialist movement in order to foster the development of viable policies that would promote the popular image of the Socialist (Labour) Party as the hope for greater social equality in Britain.[15]

The idea of elite but responsible party leadership is of course quite familiar to twentieth-century Britons. Secure in their beliefs in their own capabilities as a ruling class, Conservative spokesmen have explicitly described Tory democracy as government *of* and *for* the people, but not *by* the people. Espousing their own form of elitism, Labour leaders have often stressed that, as with union membership, it is more important to belong to the movement than to agree with every policy. While the Party Conference is supposedly the authoritative policy-making body of the Party, leaders have not bound themselves slavishly to Conference pronouncements. At times they have even called upon the rank and file to support their deviations from the official party line.[16]

In America, where the independence of elected officials is still much admired, arguments favouring responsible party government have often been challenged. The lack of discipline among elected legislators and party officials and consequent lack of coherence among party policies have been defended as highly functional responses to the demands of the great diversity of interest groups. Disciplined parties, it is argued, could not accommodate such diversity. Were strict party discipline imposed upon the Democratic and Republican parties, the two-party system would quickly come asunder, forcing the voter to choose among a confusing array of small (but disciplined) political parties, none of which stood any serious chance of assuming governmental responsibility in its own name.[17]

Not everyone has been impressed by these arguments, however. Some, such as E. E. Schattschneider, have argued that a responsible party system is necessary for the operation of a modern mass democracy. Voters can make rational choices only when parties offer them alternative programmes, well thought through, to which all the parties' nominees pledge support. For Schattschneider the requirement that the parties offer voters meaningful choices on a competitive basis is the *sine qua non* of democracy. Whether or not these choices are developed within the parties in a democratic fashion is of secondary importance. Schattschneider would undoubtedly view the recent efforts of the Democratic Party to democratize itself through the establishment of fair ratios of men to women, whites to blacks, and old to young among its national convention delegates as beside the point. The critical democratic reform, which the Democrats have failed to implement, is to gain support for the Party platform from all delegates and from all Party nominees.[18]

4

Leadership and Socialization. As revised theories of democracy, competition among interest groups or among political parties not only share elitism as a common element, they also share a common persuasion that this elitism is necessary because ordinary citizens are incapable of fulfilling the demands of liberal democracy for a rational well-informed populace. It took the ingeniousness of Joseph A. Schumpeter (1883–1950) to turn the perspective around. In *Capitalism, Socialism and Democracy*, first published in 1942, Schumpeter argued that the primary problem lay not with the citizens themselves, but with the unrealistic assumptions of the 'classical doctrine of democracy'.

This classical doctrine Schumpeter defined as:

that institutional arrangement for arriving at political decisions which realized the common good by making the people itself decide the issues through election of individuals who are to assemble in order to carry out its will.[19]

This doctrine, Schumpeter pointed out, is unrealistic in that it presumes the existence of some recognizable common good and a common will of the people to achieve it. In fact the best evidence available indicated that neither the common good nor the common will is discernible.

Schumpeter went on to point out several other fallacies in the classical doctrine. He argued, as had Mencken and Wallas, that citizens normally respond to political issues on the basis of emotion, not rational argument. Like a modern Burke, he also argued that what was rational from an individual citizen's point of view (representative of the individual citizen's opinion) was not necessarily rational from a collective one (representative of the citizen's best interest). Finally, much like Mosca, he looked at most changes of political regimes, not as the result of popular democratic movements, but as the replacement of one elite group by another.

What distinguished Schumpeter from other elitists, however, was that he went on to identify his conception of elite competition with democracy itself, not merely as a best approximation. Schumpeter boldly proposed 'another theory of democracy', one which defined the democratic method as:

that institutional arrangement for arriving at political decisions in which individuals acquire the power to decide by means of a competitive struggle for the people's vote.[20]

In effect Schumpeter's new democratic method turned the classical doctrine on its head. As he was quick to point out, his conception of democracy involved the free choice of leaders to do the governing, not the free participation of citizens in the policy-making process. Moreover, the success or failure of a democracy depended by and large upon the quality of its leadership, not upon the rationality of its ordinary citizens.

Indeed ordinary citizens needed only enough rationality to recognize the limitations of their own abilities to govern, and hence the wisdom of exercising 'Democratic Self-control'. Such self-control entailed government supporters suppressing their natural desires to pressure their representatives to pass specific policies. In Schumpeter's view sending letters, petitions, or telegrams – the traditional behaviour of good citizens – was undesirable. Self-control also entailed the opposition's confining its criticisms to constructive suggestions, which did not aim to embarrass the government.

In this democracy liberalism would be preserved through the tolerance of diversity of opinion. Such tolerance would also encourage competition among alternative sets of leaders. Nonetheless, a tendency remained even for political leaders to go too far by enacting policies which suppressed dissident opinions. To control this, Schumpeter recommended that experts or specialists be consulted on relevant problems, and that a professional bureaucracy carry out policy in accordance with its own professional ethics.

Implicit in this brave new liberal democracy is a strong faith in the democratic competence of the leaders who vie for public support to attain power to formulate, implement, and administer public policy. Yet what is the basis for this faith? The age-old question: 'Who guards the guardians?' must be answered.

Schumpeter himself was not very explicit about answering this question. He hoped that men of high quality would rise to positions of leadership, that an effective bureaucracy would curb democratic excesses, and that the leaders themselves would tolerate diversity of opinion in order to promote the very competition which allowed them to assume positions of public trust from time to time. Evidently he felt that enlightened self-interest and the process of competition itself would encourage respect for democratic processes. It took the post-Second-World-War generation of political scientists to develop a more explicit explanation – the institutions and processes of political socialization.

Political socialization – the acquisition of political norms and values by individual citizens – has burgeoned into an important field of inquiry in recent decades. The stimulus for this growth comes not only from the political scientist's curiosity about how such norms are acquired, but also from the elitist democrat's concern that leaders acquire the requisite political values to fulfil their roles as guardians of democracy. Obviously, if political leaders strive to eliminate their competition, then democracy, defined as competition among leaders, is less likely to thrive than if leaders respect their opponents' rights to compete. Former President Nixon and his advisers on the Watergate affair would not qualify as democrats, even by the most generous application of Schumpeter's revised standards.

Elitist democrats hypothesize that their version of democracy is in fact a function of the social training received by ordinary citizens, especially potential leaders.[21] The major institutions that contribute to this training are the family, the schools, peer groups, and the mass media.[22] And, happily, elitists have been able to produce a good deal of evidence that in stable democracies like the United Kingdom and the United States the social training imparted by these institutions is supportive of democratic norms.

The party identification of most citizens comes not from nature, as Gilbert and Sullivan poetically averred, but from their parents. Yet, notwithstanding these humbler origins, the effect on the polity is much the same. Each succeeding generation acquires the political loyalties and traditions of the last. This process tends to preserve a stable political system – and a democratic one too – provided that the previous generation was democratic.

And God plays His part as well, for religious identifications, even more than party loyalties, are also inherited from parents. As certain religions are predominantly loyal to one party or another, so the stability of the political system is doubly reinforced. Beyond this, in most Western countries – with an unhappy exception of Northern Ireland – the modern Judaic-Christian tradition encourages toleration of differences if not outright diversity of opinion.

Parents too are influential in providing their children with basic orientations to political issues and candidates, although, as we have seen (chapter 4), most people are largely apolitical, unconcerned about most political issues. To the extent that children develop ideas about candidates and issues, however, they are likely to reflect those of their parents. Again this is a stabilizing influence.

At age five or six, when children leave the bosom of their households to venture forth to school, they normally encounter a political atmosphere that reinforces the incipient socialization they have already received in their home. Long before they understand the political institutions the words symbolize, they have memorized the melodious strains of 'God Save the Queen' or 'My Country 'Tis of Thee'. They quickly learn of the goodness of Her Majesty or George Washington and of the benign concern the current prime minister or president has for them all. The political and social order receive high marks, even though it is usually admitted that some unfair discrimination by class and by race must still be eradicated.

To a certain extent the curriculum is tailored to suit the polity's need to justify the social and economic circumstances the young student experiences. The stress on leadership training and character building found at top-rated public schools like Eton and Harrow is hardly the norm at Shakespeare school in Maryhill, Glasgow. The working-class child must learn his place.[23] Similarly the black child from a poor family in America is more likely to learn that good citizenship entails passive acceptance of the existing political order than is his richer white contemporary.[24] In short, the schools too contribute to the stability of the democratic polity.

If a destabilizing influence enters the young citizen's political life, peer-group pressure is its most likely source. As a young citizen matures, he becomes exposed to friends and co-workers with social and political ideas different from his own. Although most social intercourse among peer-group members is devoid of political content, when circumstances do take on political significance, the citizen is likely to be receptive to the dominant political values held by the group, even when these values contradict those held by his parents and teachers.

We often recognize youthful rebellion against accepted social norms. Indeed, its starkness commands our attention. Young women bob their hair and shed their corsets; young men forsake alcohol for pot, crew cuts for hair of shoulder length. Young people develop their own argots, change their modes of dress, and scandalize their elders with their unconventional social behaviour.

But political rebellion is less easy to see. To begin with it occurs less frequently; for young people, no less than their parents, remain unconcerned about most political issues. And even when some special circumstance politicizes significant numbers of young people (as did the Vietnam War, for example), we are less apt to recognize a political rebellion than we are a social rebellion, because most of us habitually pay less attention to political than to social events.[25] Moreover, as most political values mean less to us than other values, we are less apt to become upset by a political than a social rebellion. For example, a political intermarriage normally is considerably less disturbing than racial, religious, or class intermarriage. The child who announces to his Republican parents that he is going to marry a Democrat is unlikely to cause a stir, but what about the child who announces to his white parents that he is going to marry a black? Or the young Protestant boy who falls in love with a Catholic girl? Or the young woman who decides she wants to marry someone 'beneath her station'? [26]

Yet, recognized or not, rebellion against the political values of early socialization does occur as a result of peer-group pressure. University students tend to pick up the dominant political values of their institutions. Workers come to conform to the political values of their workmates and their unions. Neighbourhoods assume particular class, religious, or racial characters, and their inhabitants tend to adopt common political orientations. On a personal level wives usually adopt the political attitudes of their husbands. And on a system-wide level the emergence of the Democratic Party as the dominant American party in the 1930s can be accounted for largely by the influx of young people, many of whose parents and teachers were Republican.[27]

Nonetheless, most political rebellion in the United States and Britain has been on the mild side. Changes in political values have proceeded slowly, and those pushing change have generally conformed to constitutionally prescribed methods for achieving it. In the past generation blacks, Indians, Chicanos, and other racially oppressed American minorities have never resorted to terrorism. In Britain neither have the Welsh or Scots in pressing their nationalist claims. Northern Ireland remains an unfortunate and incompletely accounted for exception.[28]

The mass media, the fourth major influence on socialization, also reinforce the dominant political values of the polity. Although the public tends to pay the most attention to the issues the media emphasize; although most of the public's information about politics in general comes from these sources; studies show over and over again that not only do the political values of most popular media reflect those of the dominant groups in the polity, but citizens tend to be receptive only to those values which already conform to their own. The media's contribution to political socialization is largely reinforcement, not conversion.[29]

5

Critiques of the Revised Theories. As mentioned at the outset of this chapter, these revised theories of democracy comprise the major contribution post-war political science has made to the development of normative political theory. Where the works of Truman, Schattschneider, and Schumpeter pioneered the idea that competition among interest groups, political parties, or leadership elites was the essence of democracy, the succeeding studies of empirical political scientists quickly settled the intellectual ground. By the mid sixties the case for elitist democracy had been well established.

The most influential post-war statement of the elitist thesis was developed by Bernard Berelson, Paul Lazarsfeld and William McPhee as the concluding chapter of their now classic study, *Voting*.[30] The argument of that chapter – that energetic political participation by ordinary citizens is harmful to democratic government – was represented as a necessary consequence of the carefully developed empirical findings of the earlier chapters. As methods and findings of these earlier chapters became the inspiration for many subsequent studies, the elitist argument of the concluding chapter was carried along almost as an afterthought.[31]

To begin with Berelson *et al.* demonstrated conclusively that the average citizens in their study fell far short of the standards of conscientious and knowledgeable participation set by our mythical Good Citizen Brown. But even if the average citizen were to participate with all the zeal of the good citizen, the authors contended that the results would still be unsatisfactory. Persistent high levels of political participation would produce deadlock at best and social breakdown at worst, for such political participation inevitably leads to polarization of large blocs of citizens around highly emotional issues. Far better to achieve a balance – a few highly motivated citizens; a few apoliticals. The rest should become part of a grand coalition, a happy centre group whose individual members were interested only sporadically in a variety of political issues, but who supported in common the rules and institutions of the polity.[32]

While conceding that this view of democracy failed to coincide with other more idealistic ones, Berelson *et al.* argued that it had the advantage of being realistic. In their view the United States was a democracy. And if its citizens did not act in accordance with the empirical assumptions postulated in some normative theories of democracy, then the fault lay with the theories, not with the citizenry. Accordingly, democratic theory ought to be modified to correspond to the realities of citizens' behaviour.

William Kornhauser and Seymour Martin Lipset made parallel arguments after reviewing a large body of empirical data on mass behaviour in Western industrial states. Both men concluded that direct political participation by the masses too often led to breakdowns of liberal-democratic processes and to the institution of totalitarian regimes. In the *Politics of Mass Society* (1959) Kornhauser laid great emphasis on the role of secondary groups acting as buffers between the ruling elites and the masses. In a democratic system the elites receive their cues from public demands expressed not from individual citizens directly, but through interest groups and parties in an organized manner. At the same time the secondary groups provide the individual citizens with protection against unscrupulous manipulation by the elites.[33] In *Political Man* (1959) Lipset too emphasized the stabilizing influences of voluntary associations in a democratic state. In his view higher levels of economic development of the society and higher socio-economic status of the individual citizens encouraged greater numbers of voluntary associations; and contact with such associations in turn encouraged orderly politics and discouraged extremism by exposing members to competing sources of information.[34] For both men the absence of a strong system of voluntary associations was the prelude to dictatorship.

By the early 1960s the elitist modifications came thick and fast with the burgeoning numbers of empirical studies concerning public opinion. Among the more prominent studies Peter J. G. Pulzer's *Political Representation and Elections* (1967) extended the balanced-democracy argument to the United Kingdom.[35] Gabriel Almond and Sidney Verba pushed it even further in the *Civic Culture* (1963), by citing Berelson's argument as the basis for concluding that characteristics of a democratic *Civic*

Culture were prevalent in Great Britain and the United States, and were also present, though to a lesser extent, in West Germany, Italy and Mexico. In the end the concept of a 'Civic Culture' bore an acknowledged resemblance to the balanced democracy of *Voting*.[36]

Party competition was championed as the basis for democracy by E. E. Schattschneider in the United States and Robert McKenzie in Great Britain. In the *Semi-Sovereign People* (1960) Schattschneider used the new data on the effects of party loyalty on voting behaviour to place flesh on his long-held bone of contention that modern democracy was nothing more and nothing less than the product of party competition.[37] In *British Political Parties* (1954) McKenzie, like a latter day Michels, marshalled evidence showing that despite their differing philosophies the internal power structures of the Labour and Conservative parties were remarkably similar.[38] In both parties the leadership exerted a dominant influence over the membership. McKenzie concluded that democracy in Britain stemmed from competition between the parties, not within them.

Finally, as if to harmonize with the grand Tory tradition in Britain, American political scientists like V. O. Key and Herbert McClosky proceeded to extol leadership itself as the basis of democracy. After a thorough-going analysis of the empirical political literature, Key concluded his *Public Opinion and American Democracy* (1961) with the proposition that:

> The longer one frets with puzzle of how democratic régimes manage to function, the more plausible it appears that a substantial part of the explanation is to be found in the motives that actuate the leadership echelon, the values that it holds, in the rules of the political game to which it adheres ... and perhaps, in some of the objective circumstances, both material and institutional, in which it functions.[39]

McClosky, in 'Consensus And Ideology in American Politics', (1964), went on to demonstrate afresh that in comparison with the masses, party leaders subscribed more completely to the values of liberal democracy.[40] Better to place faith in the democratic predilections of the leaders than in whims of the people, these authors implied.

As they were based upon the new wave of scientifically generated studies of political behaviour, these elitist interpretations of democratic theory gained widespread acceptance among the new generation of empirically oriented political scientists. Beyond this, the self-congratulatory tone of the elitists' arguments – democracy was an accomplished fact, the common good sure to emerge from the clash of parties and interests – made them popular with students of politics and the general reading public. By the mid 1960s these interpretations under the broad label of pluralism, had become dominant themes presented in major introductory political science textbooks, particularly those on American government.[41]

Yet despite the popular acceptance of pluralist-elitist interpretations of democracy, some nagging questions remained about the actual governance of Western societies. And these questions eventually led to some devastating criticisms of the adequacy of these interpretations.

If the political system were as democratic as proclaimed, then every significant interest in society ought to have a fair chance to present its case to the ruling elite, or to compete for positions of power within that elite. Yet if every interest really had a fair chance, then why did systematic patterns of discrimination persist against minority racial and religious groups, women, the poor, and others in such diverse areas as housing, educational opportunity, health care, and employment? If the political system were sensitive to each group's needs, then what caused blacks of America's urban ghettoes to riot? If organized political activity were the *sine qua non* of elitist democracy, then why did America's political leaders treat organized opposition to the immoral and increasingly unpopular war in Vietnam as though it were illegitimate? If the clash of parties and interests led to the emergence of policies in the public interest, then how did one account for Britain's troubles in Northern Ireland? In short the actual governance of Britain and the United States did not comport with the empirical expectations of elitist theories of democracy.

Towards the end of the 1960s considerations of this sort resulted in a multi-faceted critique of the revised theories, a critique attacking them on both empirical and philosophical grounds.

Let us first examine the empirical grounds of this critique.

In its actual operation democracy as the interaction of diverse interest groups excludes a large number of potential participants. In the United States, for instance, an estimated 40 per cent of the adult population belongs to no voluntary associations whatsoever. And only about half of those who belong to such associations see them as having any concern with community problems.[42] For the United Kingdom the comparable proportions of participants in group activities are even smaller. About half the adult population claims membership in community organizations, and only about 20 per cent describe their membership as 'active'.[43]

Such low figures prove little in themselves. Any defender of group-related theories of democracy could point out that low participation does not discredit his arguments; it tends to reinforce them. The activities of groups are, after all, *supposed* to substitute for the individual citizen's own participation. The important point is that each citizen's interests are represented either through a currently active interest group or a potentially active one which can easily be actualized in a democratic society. Thus lack of participation on the part of citizens can be viewed as voluntary, and it can be interpreted as a sign of public satisfaction, a tacit endorsement of the current public policies.

But the fact is that membership in voluntary associations is highly biased. Producer groups, for instance, far outstrip consumer groups in resources and number. An extra penny for a loaf of bread or a gallon of petrol means a lot more to the bakers or the oil producers than it does to the average consumer. Thus the producers, for whom the extra pennies add up to millions, are far more willing to devote time and resources to furthering their interests than are consumers. Moreover, as we shall later discuss (chapter 6), the tax structures of modern industrial states subsidize many of the political activities of producer groups, allowing them to deduct the costs of lobbying and public relations, for example, as legitimate business expenses. In contrast, consumer groups normally receive no such subsidies.

Labour groups, too, tend to look out for the interests of their members in their roles as workers, not as consumers. Concern for wages and working conditions does not usually include how the conditions of the environment surrounding the workplace or factory are affected, nor does it consider the ability of the company to pass its increased labour costs on to the consumer. Nor are labour groups necessarily representative of all employees in the workforce. Not only is union membership unevenly distributed across industries – nearly all workers in some industries are organized; in others, nearly none – but overall, about half the employees in Britain and more than half of those in the United States can claim no union representation whatsoever.[44]

Over and above the bias in the composition of the interests that are organized, there is bias in the class membership of groups. Those of lower socio-economic status – whether measured by income, occupation, education or any combination of these – tend to be excluded from participation. On the average those of low status possess neither the wherewithal to participate at rates comparable to more affluent compatriots nor the forensic or manipulative skills that effective participation in such groups requires. In fact to the extent that political scientists have studied them, the political attitudes held by lower-status activists have been found different from those held by ordinary members of their class.[45]

For that matter, as pointed out by Michels so long ago, group leaders, lower status or otherwise, tend to form a class apart from their followers. Even among well-organized affluent groups, initiative normally devolves from followers to leaders. After groups have become well-established the modern leader often adopts an entrepreneurial role, seeking out projects and policies around which he can mobilize his members' support. In addition leaders try to develop policies and programmes with exclusive benefits for group members only, the better to maintain loyalty and to encourage continued membership.[46]

Finally, for good or for ill, the clash of interest groups leads to a politics of bargaining and compromise. Such a politics has the virtue of stability, incremental changes gradually accumulating until their cumulative effects are recognized as substantial changes in policy. But such a politics has its vices as well; for it is conceivable that political problems could arise which demand radical solutions, problems for which the gradualism of compromise is particularly ill-suited. For instance the deterioration of natural environment through industrial pollution and exploitation of natural resources may call for radical changes in public policies currently devoted to encouraging expansion of the industrial base. As the dominant labour and industrial groups have a vested interest in increased production, it is difficult to conceive of any changes in policy occurring until a total collapse of the ecological system appears imminent. By then it may be too late for any measures to succeed, radical or otherwise.

Party politics suffers from many of the same short-comings as interest-group politics. Even though, in comparison with interest groups, larger proportions of Britons and Americans belong to or at least identify with the major political parties of their respective countries, substantial proportions do not. And, judging by the evidence of recent public-opinion polls, these proportions are growing.[47] Moreover, as with interest groups, a disproportionately large number of middle-class individuals become leaders and, like the leaders in interest groups, these leaders tend to ignore the interests of the least well-organized segments of the population.

But even if it were plausible that the major parties in the United States and Britain provided the voters with alternative sets of leaders broadly subscribing to alternative sets of principles and policies, the fact remains that over the past twenty years the alternatives offered by the parties have become increasingly irrelevant to the central concerns of the citizenry. In 1972, for instance, the Survey Research Center of the University of Michigan found that 41 per cent of their national sample saw no differences between the Democrats and Republicans regarding the most important problem citizens thought government should act upon. In 1964 only 21 per cent saw no difference.[48] The decline in turnout in national elections in the United States – from 62 per cent in 1960, to 52 per cent in 1976 – has been interpreted by political scientists like Norman Nie, Sidney Verba, and W. D. Burnham as a manifest indication of the irrelevance of party choices and the disgust of large numbers of voters with the party system.[49] In studying British national elections, Ivor Crewe has given a similar interpretation to the declining proportions of the eligible electors' votes, which the Labour and Conservative parties have received since the Second World War.[50] In short the recent evidence suggests the parties are rather shaky pillars upon which to rest the edifice of democracy.

Nor does recent evidence on democratic traits of political leaders lend much credence to the argument that these people can be counted upon to uphold democratic values more surely than will ordinary citizens. As was pointed out in the preceding chapter, recent studies in Glasgow and Belfast found no significant differences between city councillors and ordinary electors regarding questions of majority rule and minority rights. In addition recent studies by Robert Jackman and others have suggested that social-class differences between leaders and followers, not political socialization to leadership roles, account for the differences in support for democratic values found between leaders and followers.[51] Finally we should note again that, far from having no rational justification, the cynicism many ordinary citizens have regarding the motives, honesty, and democratic *bona fides* of their leaders arises from bitter experience: too many politicians not only lie, cheat, and steal but, when they are found out, they try to suppress those who have exposed them.[52]

While the empirical critique raises severe doubts about the adequacy of relying upon groups, parties, or leaders to effect democracy, the philosophical critique argues that the concept of democracy as described by revisionists is itself inadequate. Thus, even if groups, parties, and leaders functioned in the manner revisionists describe, the resultant polity would not be a liberal democracy.

To begin with revisionists formulate an impoverished conception of democratic citizenship. They abandon the traditional liberal concern for individual self-improvement, particularly that achieved through political participation. Instead these theorists presume that given the proper social arrangements the virtues of political leaders can be substituted for the virtues of the people Are the citizens too lazy or indifferent to decide intelligently about questions of public policy? No matter: the leaders of groups representing their interest will decide for them. Are the citizens ignorant of the major issues of the day? No matter: the political parties will reduce all the complexities to a simple choice among alternative slates of candidates. Are the citizens motivated only by selfish concerns? Are they intolerant of those with whom they disagree? No matter: the leadership elite has a benign concern for the rights and privileges of all the citizenry. The political life of such a citizenry is hardly the rich one envisaged by men like Jefferson, Rousseau, or Mill.

This impoverished conception of citizenship rests upon an emasculated conception of liberal democracy itself. For revisionists, democracy in the United States, Britain and other Western nations is already in operation. Their concern then becomes how to *preserve* democracy rather than how to *achieve* it. To this end they frankly admit their fear of rapid or radical changes in policies or procedures. Revisionists prefer gradual changes arrived at through negotiations among leaders of parties and interest groups; they fear social movements that shun these established channels and attempt to mobilize citizens for direct political participation.[53]

Yet, as we have argued, the primary object of government in a liberal democracy is to maintain open the widest range of options and values for its citizens. Not only must there be no premature closure of alternatives, but any set of chosen alternatives must be viewed as impermanent, constantly open to challenge. Change, not stability, is the watchword of liberal democrats. And as far as liberal democrats are concerned, change may be abrupt or gradual, for their faith in the ultimate rationality and good will of ordinary citizens leads them to expect orderly change and harmonious outcomes. If, as hard-headed revisionists argue, such faith in ordinary Britons or Americans is not empirically justified, then Britain and America are not yet liberal democracies.

In fact revisionists are not really democrats at all. Philosophically they are Hobbesian liberals, elitists with little faith in the capacity of ordinary men to govern themselves. Like Hobbes they emphasize stability and order as prerequisites for any individual self-development. As they are modern revisionists, however, they transcend mere personal observations to justify their lack of faith. They turn instead to the findings of contemporary political science. And instead of proposing surrender of all power to the Leviathan they entrust political power to competing groups of elites. Members of these elites, as it turns out, are drawn disproportionately from higher status men and women as are the revisionists themselves.[54]

6

Conclusions: In spite of their apparent relevance, when the first critiques of revisionist theories appeared in the late 50s and early 60s, they made little impact. Why was this so?

First, the critiques of democratic theory were usually buried in larger tracts, devoted mostly to condemning the entire enterprise of political science. Where pointed essays were called for, critics produced mostly broadsides. Early critics argued not merely that certain considerations about democratic values were ignored by empirical scientists, but that the whole attempt to discover regular patterns of political participation through systematic study was futile – or if not futile, then immoral in purpose – a threat to the exercise of free will.[55] The attacks were so sweeping, their tone so strident, that most political scientists simply dismissed them as preposterous and continued with their (futile and immoral) research.

Secondly, in the late 50s and early 60s the governments of Britain and the United States, dubbed pluralist democracies by the revisionists, functioned well. Britain 'never had it so good' in 1959. And America entered the 'soaring sixties' with unbounded optimism, her forward-looking President the first born in the twentieth century. In general Britain and America prospered. The energy crisis, pollution, and runaway inflation were unheard of. Even world peace seemed possible: EFTA and the EEC were formed; the Peace Corps begun; the nuclear test ban treaty signed. Catholic resentments seethed only in Stormont; not yet had they boiled over into the streets of Belfast. Black anger smouldered quietly in the ghettos; not yet had it flamed in the streets of Newark, Detroit or Los Angeles. With things going so well few felt the need to re-examine the fundamental values and assumptions upon which the conduct of government was based.

By the late 1960s, however, the critiques gained more force. By then it was clear that pluralist democracy had not worked out so well. In Britain the pound had been devalued and unemployment had risen. The troubles in Northern Ireland had begun again, and there had been a sudden resurgence of the Scottish and Welsh nationalist parties. In America the Vietnam war had escalated to proportions which threatened not only domestic economic programmes but domestic tranquillity too. Domestic violence became standard fare on the evening news as well as the war. Nor was the economy doing well: unemployment and inflation increased simultaneously, an occurrence without precedent. If pluralist democracy was the best of all possible governments, why did it produce such disastrous public policy? Political scientists and others began to feel a greater willingness to return to fundamental considerations of the conduct of government.

The newer critics faced a more receptive professional audience, therefore, than had their predecessors. But they presented better arguments as well. These new men shared with the revisionists a sophisticated appreciation of the accomplishments and the promise of empirical political science. Thus while they could concede the importance of the revisionists' descriptions of the shortcomings of the ordinary citizen, they could nevertheless point out the dangers of equating with democracy a polity whose citizens displayed such shortcomings.[56]

The impact of the criticisms of revisionist theories of democracy is clearly seen if we compare contemporary American government textbooks with those of the 1960s. Almost without exception the latter subscribe to pluralist notions of democracy. Their discussions of democratic theory read like panegyrics on American society – with a few minor caveats appended concerning the plight of the 'Negro'. In contrast the contemporary textbooks are far more critical. Commonly subtitled 'Promise and Performance' or some similar phrase implying critical scrutiny, some even suggest anti-democratic trends, *e.g. The Perverted Priorities of American Politics.*[57] Inside they document the denial of equal opportunity to blacks, Indians, women, and other underprivileged groups. And they ponder whether or not this discrimination is a necessary consequence of the form competition takes among American political elites.

Even in Britain, where leadership by established elites is buttressed by habit and tradition, some new textbooks raise doubts about the responsiveness of these elites to the needs of the people. These texts advocate more policy input from ordinary citizens. To this end they recommend greater devolution of power from central government to local regions; or they suggest placing greater reliance for policy initiative upon the people's representatives in Parliament and less upon the Government and its advisory boards.[58]

As we pointed out in the beginning, despite their success in uncovering the deficiences in revised theories of democracy, nearly all the critiques lack one crucial element: they offer no positive statement about how political institutions and processes can be arranged so that citizens can cope with the responsibilities of contemporary government in accordance with the liberal-democratic tradition. By now it should be clear as well that any such statement must take into account not only empirical evidence on the capabilities of the average citizen, as did the revised theories, but also the philosophical values contained in classical statements of democratic theory.

But the problem is more difficult yet. In addition to satisfying the above requirements, any positive statement of liberal-democratic theory must take into account new actors and new conditions that impinge upon the conduct of twentieth-century government. These include the immense military and civilian bureaucracies operated by government, the huge and powerful multinational corporations that influence government, and the enormous ecological problems that increasingly restrict the range of policy choices available to government. Before proceeding to our promised development of a theory of viable democracy, therefore, it becomes necessary to discuss these new actors and conditions in some detail. To this task the next chapter is devoted.

6 · The Death of Democracy

Nowadays the members of Parliament, with the exception of a few cabinet members (and a few insurgents) are normally nothing better than well-disciplined 'yes' men.
Max Weber, *Politics as a Vocation*, 1919; Fortress Press, 1965.

The ease with which global corporations can conceal or distort information for the management of the economy is creating the same sort of administrative nightmare for the advanced industrial state that under-developed countries have lived with for years ... Their political power stems from their ability to sprinkle more cash at campaign time, when the regulators are running for office, and to supply from their own ranks a generous number of commissioners and assistant secretaries to the regulatory process regardless of which party is in power.
Richard Barnett and Ronald Müller, *Global Reach*, Simon & Shuster, 1974.

... threats of runaway populations, obliterative war, and potential environmental collapse, can be seen as an extended and growing crisis by the advent of a command over natural processes and forces that far exceeds the reach of our present mechanism of social control ... Yet, candor compels me to suggest that the passage through the gauntlet ahead may be possible only under governments capable of rallying obedience far more effectively than would be possible in a democratic setting.
Robert Heilbroner, *An Inquiry into the Human Prospect*, W. W. Norton & Co., 1974.

I

Introduction. The popularly elected legislature has long been cited as the cornerstone of liberal-democratic polities. Indeed in

Considerations on Representative Government John Stuart Mill even went so far as to argue that once the masses were enfranchised the 'ideally best polity' was a representative government.[1] Moreover, the last decades of the nineteenth century saw not only the extension of the franchise, but the dominance of the legislature. From 1833 to 1867 the Commons exerted itself in no mean fashion, dismissing some seven governments outright. (Three others were defeated when they 'went to the country' seeking a new parliamentary majority.) And in the United States the Congress exercised its muscle first by impeaching Lincoln's successor, Andrew Johnson, in 1868, and then by dominating subsequent presidents at least until Theodore Roosevelt assumed office in 1901.

It is widely recognized that twentieth-century legislatures have declined in power relative to the executive. The bureaucracy of the executive has played an increasingly dominant role in the formulation of public policy, particularly since the advent of government economic planning and the welfare state. Over and above this the military and the major corporations have come to play increasingly important roles in the public-policy process, roles not only free of most control from the legislature, but also in many aspects free from interference by the executive.

And as if the unprecedented growth of the executive, the military, and the private corporations were not enough to rock the foundations of liberal democracy, the earth itself has trembled beneath the economic burden liberal democrats have placed upon it. Individual self-development, self-expression and self-aggrandizement – traditional goals of liberal-democratic polities – presume a nearly inexhaustible supply of raw materials from which free men may fashion their fortunes. For that matter socialist theories also presume that science and technology can provide mankind with the wherewithal to fashion ideal social orders. Yet shortages of food, minerals, and energy, not to mention immense problems of environmental pollution, which stem from exploitation of the remaining natural resources, cast into doubt the correctness of these presumptions. And if they rest upon unrealistic presumptions, how viable are the visions of liberal-democratic or even socialist societies?

In this chapter we look at these new threats to liberal democracy more closely. We begin by examining the new political entities which constrain traditional democratic institutions. This leads to an examination of the environmental factors, which constrain not only traditional institutions but the new political entities as well.

2

The decline of legislatures. In the spring of 1973 whilst young men's fancies turned to love, so too did the thoughts of their legislators. By a vote of 118 to 69 the Pennsylvania House of Representatives passed a bill making fornication within the state of Pennsylvania a crime. The provisions outlawing fornication were passed as a rider to a bill which declared malicious mischief in caves a misdemeanour.[2]

Now we may question the ability of the state to prevent by law a voluntary act between two consenting parties; more broadly, we may question the wisdom of even attempting to legislate morality: and we may also point out the probable hypocrisy of numerous legislators who supported the bill – yet we would be forced to concede that reasonable men might differ on the subject of legislating against fornication. It would be utterly preposterous to conclude, however, that reasonable men would see any obvious connection between malicious mischief in caves and fornication. That such arrant nonsense should emanate from 187 presumably rational representatives of the people may say more about legislative institutions and their procedures than about the legislators themselves.

Yet if legislative procedures have gone awry, then liberal democracy is in trouble. The most strenuous act of political participation for approximately half the adult citizens of Britain and America consists of nothing more than casting their ballots at election time. And whom do the citizens elect? Mostly their representatives to local, regional, and national legislatures. In parliamentary systems like the British citizens never elect the executive directly. And even in presidential systems like the American, citizens ordinarily do not elect most of the top officers of the executive. Nor are judges – even elected judges who are common at the state and local levels in the United States – supposed to serve directly as the representatives of the people in the policy-making process. Only the popularly elected legislator remains central to most conceptions of liberal democracy. How else will most citizens be afforded an opportunity to participate?

Unfortunately legislatures are far less viable today than they were at the turn of the century. Even though they are usually in session longer, and even though they pass laws which affect citizens' lives more profoundly, the fact remains that relative to the executive, twentieth-century legislatures have grown weaker. Why has this happened? Because the tasks modern government performs have become increasingly more technical and specialized. These tasks often require knowledge and expertise that go beyond the mastery of the ordinary legislative generalist, but lie within the specialized competence of the bureaucratic expert. The day when President Andrew Jackson could plausibly argue that the tasks of government were so simple that any citizen of ordinary intelligence could administer them is long behind us.

Consider an example: street cleaning, one of the earliest services provided by urban government. In the early 1800s the service consisted mainly of removal of the horse manure and household slops from the main thoroughfares. No complicated or expensive equipment was required, just a few carts, shovels and brooms. The garbage and other debris were gathered up and carted to the city dump. The city fathers, who met only infrequently, could nonetheless oversee this operation, for not only was it straightforward, but it also represented a major portion of all the services for which government was responsible. Today street cleaning is but one of an ever-growing number of services provided by the city. And it has become more complex and more expensive. To start with, as there are now more streets to clean, there is more discretion allowed in deciding which streets should be cleaned. Further considerations include how often each street should be cleaned and the order in which they should be cleaned. What equipment should be used, and in what combination? Should the refuse be dumped or recycled in some way? Should street cleaning be integrated with household refuse collection or other sanitation services? And in budgetary considerations what priority should street-cleaning receive in relation to other services? Clearly, even though its features have not become inordinately complex, legislative oversight of street cleaning is a more difficult task today than it was in the 1800s.

We need only multiply these difficulties by the manifold services national governments now undertake to provide, in order to appreciate the enormity of the tasks of modern legislative governance. Being a Member of Parliament or of Congress has already become a full-time job, and being a member of lesser legislative bodies is becoming increasingly demanding of time. It is no accident that as legislative elections have been democratized through extension of the franchise to all classes, so, too, legislatures have become professionalized, through extension of substantial salaries to their members. Legislating has become so time consuming that, without salaries, only the independently wealthy or those sponsored by the wealthy could afford to serve.

Yet even professional legislators do not possess sufficient expertise for effective legislative governance. For just as the responsibilities of government have become too diverse for the average citizen to comprehend, so the administration of legislation has become too complex for the average legislator to control. The power to administer, plan, propose, and even to promulgate legislation has increasingly devolved from the legislature to the bureaucracy, and in many cases from the upper echelons of the bureaucracy to middle-level positions occupied by technically competent professional civil servants. To be sure, legislators have reorganized themselves in order to cope better with the bureaucrats – they have formed specialized committees; they have developed comprehensive party programmes – but they have not recovered control.

Nor are they likely to under the present institutional arrangements. Even the institutional resources of the Congress of the United States, reputedly the most powerful legislature of the Western industrial states, are dwarfed by those of the bureaucracy it ostensibly oversees. Counting its vaunted specialized committees and their staffs, individual members' staffs, and the staff of the General Accounting Office, the manpower Congress had directly at its disposal totalled 21·3 thousand in 1974. (The entire legislative branch, including the staffs of the Library of Congress, the Government Printing Office, and the Architect of the Capitol totalled 36·5 thousand.) In contrast the executive branch employed some 2·8 million civilians, not to mention another 2·1 million in uniform. At that time President Nixon alone employed a staff of 5,800 in his Executive Office. By comparison the staffs of both the General Accounting Office and the Library of Congress numbered less than this figure, and the entire payroll of the United States Senate barely exceeded it. To his credit Gerald Ford drastically reduced the size of the Executive Office, thus scotching for the nonce one aspect of the 'Imperial Presidency'. (See Table 3). The dollar amounts allocated for personnel of each branch were commensurately lopsided: $37,935 million to the executive, $519 million to the legislative. Overall the executive branch accounted for 91·6 per cent of the $268 billion spent by the federal government in 1974; the legislative branch spent only $625 million, barely 0·2 per cent. (An additional $21·5 billion went towards interest on the National Debt.)

Now the disparity of resources in itself would not guarantee executive predominance, but the manner of employment of these resources does. Since 1933, and especially since the Second World War, the executive has managed to seize the policy-making initiative. Using its superior sources of manpower and information the executive has not only taken over the budgetary initiative, it has also taken to drafting legislative programmes and to supplying major inputs of information in support of those programmes. Moreover, in many policy areas, particularly national defence, the Congress has been powerless to generate alternative sources of information which might possibly contradict the executive's presentation and or interpretation of that information. In the last resort the executive has shielded its information on national defence from congressional scrutiny by evoking the privilege of secrecy in the name of national security. For other policy areas it has adopted a similar tactic: secrecy in the name of executive

Table 3 U.S. Federal Government: Selected Employment, Payrolls, and Expenditures 1960-75

Employment (thousands)

	General Accounting Office	Library of Congress	Senate	Congress	Executive Office of President	HEW	Veteran Admin. (VA)	Defence	Civilian Executive	Military*
1975	5·5	4·6	6·1	17·3	1·9	147·1	213·1	1,023·2	2,848·0	2,084
1974	5·2	4·5	5·7	16·0	5·7	142·2	202·3	1,041·8	2,847·1	2,140
1970	4·6	3·8	4·4	11·8	4·7	108·0	168·7	1,193·8	2,884·3	2,874
1965	4·3	3·4	3·5	9·3	2·8	87·3	167·1	1,033·8	2,495·6	2,857
1960	5·1	2·8	2·8	7·1	2·9	61·6	172·3	1,047·1	2,370·4	2,494

Payrolls (millions of dollars)

	Congress	Executive	Military (active only)
1975	460	39,944	21,200
1974	410	36,935	20,600
1970	250	28,117	19,400
1965	99	17,746	11,400
1960	68	13,052	9,300

Expenditures (millions of dollars)

	Total	Legislative Branch	Executive† Branch	HEW	VA	Defence	Defence Contracts
1975	324,601	726	323,540	112,411	16,505	87,071	43,355
1974	268,392	625	267,534	93,735	13,874	79,307	37,760
1970	196,600	343	196,117	68,382	8,952	77,148	35,977
1965	118,400	165	118,152	31,701	6,011	46,173	27,997
1960	92,200	126	92,018	19,590	5,367	41,215	23,689

SOURCES: *Statistical Abstract of the United States, 1976* Bureau of Census, Washington, D.C., 1976, tables 374, 406, 459, 513, 525, 527, 531; *Budget of the United States Government* (1977, 1976, 1972, 1967, 1961), U.S. Government Printing Office, Washington, D.C., annually; *Combined Statement of Receipts Expenditures and Balance of the United States Government* (fiscal years 1960, 1965, 1970, 1974, 1975), US Treasury Dept., Washington DC, annually.
*3·4 million in 1968. †Excluding interest on National Debt.

131

privilege. Only when the Watergate scandals revealed just how far the executive under Mr Nixon had overstepped its legitimate authority, did the Congress take some serious steps to strengthen its ability to criticize and change the President's budget and to otherwise reserve more policy-making initiatives for itself.

And if the Congress has been largely ineffectual in curbing executive power, how much more ineffectual has been the Parliament? In 1975 ordinary backbench and opposition members had no offices, no personal staff, few specialized committees, and little funding even for secretarial help. The entire Commons budget amounted to a mere £8·4 million of £26·2 milliards in central government expenditures.[3] Faced with this situation most members of Parliament have been forced to become what Weber rather disparagingly described as 'well disciplined "yes" men'.

Yet, given their weakened institutional situation, the backbenchers' shift in emphasis from specific and detailed legislative directives to the broad policy pronouncements of the party programme makes a good deal of sense. With its superior resources the executive can usually overwhelm legislative opposition on any specific proposal. But if Members of Parliament get a hand in the formulation of the party programme, for instance through meetings of the party caucus or through prominent roles in the Annual Party Conference, then the programme and its attendant party discipline allows for some legislative control. Even the boldest executive is loath to propose legislation which contradicts its own party programme.

And though legislators cannot control most actions of the bureaucracy, they can act as Ombudsmen for particular constituents, to humanize the decisions of the bureaucracy and to ameliorate their detrimental effects. Legislators in the United States typically spend over half their time servicing their constituents' requests. In Britain MPs not only act informally on behalf of their constituents but they also require that all formal requests to the Parliamentary Commissioner (Ombudsman) be channelled through a Member of Parliament.[4] Question time is also used to air specific grievances of constituents, often to greater effect than to criticize government policy.[5] Moreover, at election the rewards for constituency service are frequently greater than those received for legislating. After all, most voters are concerned more about how policies and decisions affect them personally than about how such policies and decisions affect the polity.

As previously mentioned, specialization can be used to develop sufficient expertise to criticize and control gross abuses of administration. Congress has a longstanding tradition of specialized committees which scrutinize both legislative proposals and administration of laws in their areas of competence; Parliament, since 1966, has moved in this direction through the expansion of the numbers and powers of its specialized select committees. Legislative specialization by disparate committees, however, does not provide the legislature with the coordinated planning capabilities of the executive. The legislature authors no programme. The initiative remains largely with the President or Prime Minister.

Given these institutional constraints, what sorts of issues are likely to lend themselves to legislative initiatives? Those with the following features: 1) a high saliency for a significant group of representatives' constituents; 2) a high symbolic value for the polity as a whole; and 3) no direct relevance for partisan party politics. Fornication fits the bill – so do issues like abortion, birching, hanging, and pornography and curbing political corruption and waste of government funds.

Unfortunately, even on these issues legislatures have not been notably successful. Some of this is excusable: by their very nature many issues of morality are almost irresolvable, for legislated standards nearly always impose a level of conformity which significant numbers of citizens find intolerable. Thus much of the effort to legislate morality performs a cathartic function for the polity, even though it produces little of lasting substance. But legislative efforts to curb waste and corruption tend to focus on niggling examples: a few thousands of the taxpayers' monies spent on junketing or philandering often receive more attention than many millions wasted on the Blue Streak or TFX-1. A welfare recipient who gets away with an extra hundred is reviled more than a government contractor whose cost overruns are enormous. Legislators as well as their constituents more readily comprehend small-scale corruption of the crudest sort than large-scale corruption of a more refined nature.

3

The military. Even more than the civilian bureaucracy, however, the military bureaucracy defies legislative control. The growth of the military since the Second World War poses a fundamental dilemma for democratic government. On the one hand the weaponry of modern warfare can be employed with such awesome efficiency that no nation can defend itself from a surprise attack without a substantial armed force at the ready. Consequently governments have been obliged to devote massive amounts of manpower, treasure, and scientific research to military defence. On the other hand devoting so many resources to the armed forces inevitably increases the danger that the military elite, not the people or their representatives, will ultimately determine the choices made in crucial areas of public policy. Why is this so?

It follows from a cardinal rule of organizational behaviour: bureaucrats will act to preserve, protect, and expand the programmes they administer.[6] And in the case of the military, the bureaucrats find themselves in a particularly advantageous position. First, no one can gainsay their ultimate purpose: the protection of the life and property of the citizenry. Secondly to be credible, any military defence must involve substantial outlays of resources. Thirdly much of the weaponry involved is of a highly technical variety, difficult for the layman to understand but suited to the capacities of the bureaucratic expert. Finally, so central are the military's purposes to the survival of the nation that, lest a potential enemy detect a weakness, much of the information critical to making a judgement about the armed forces' true preparedness and their efficiency must remain secret.

The might of the military bureaucracy is itself quite formidable. The interests of the 2·1 million men and women still in uniform in the United States after the Vietnam War in mid 70s, for instance, were looked after by over one million civilian employees in the defence department, while another 213,000 civilian employees looked after the interests of former soldiers through their work in the Veterans Administration (see Table 3). Despite the growth of the Welfare State, civilian employees of both the aforementioned agencies outnumbered the 147,000 employees of the Department of Health, Education and Welfare (HEW). The actual outlays for Fiscal 1975 totalled $324·6 billion. Of this Defense received $87·0 billion, Veterans $16·6 billion, while an additional $23·3 billion went for interest, mostly war debts. Excluding war debt, however, HEW outspent Defense and Veterans in Fiscal 1975.

Nonetheless, the nature of Defense Department expenditures makes them especially useful as bargaining chips with the Congress. Of the $87 billion available in 1975, some $43·3 billion was awarded as contracts for supplies, services and construction. As many of these contracts are for highly specialized products, the Department normally gets a good deal of leeway to negotiate with selected contractors, rather than simply having to let the contracts to the lowest bidder. But which contractor should get the awards? And in whose legislative districts should the work take place? It is very hard for a Congressman to question the wisdom of a technical decision, based in part upon classified information, which happens to deny his district any contracts. It is easier to go along with the Defense Department's budgetary requests with the tacit understanding that such support will be remembered when the Department distributes its largesse.[7]

By way of contrast HEW has much less flexibility with its expenditures. Of $112 billion spent in 1975, $78 billion was mandated to be distributed in dribs and drabs to individuals as Old-Age, Survivors and Disability Insurance Benefits (OASDI), and substantial portions of the remaining money went out in the form of Medicare, Medicaid or public-welfare-formula payments to the states. In all, nearly 90 per cent of HEW's annual expenditures take the form of inflexible payments mandated by law.[8]

Defence and Welfare expenditures differ in one other important aspect. Expenditures of the sort made by HEW are far easier for Congressmen and the general public to scrutinize than are those of the military. It is easier for a layman to comprehend that through connivance Joe Bloggs and 3,000 others like him have each received overpayments of $100. It is far more difficult to comprehend that through mismanagement the army has lost several hundred million dollars of supplies and capital equipment shipped to Vietnam. The mind boggles at contemplating such gross amounts – far more money than most citizens earn in a life time. Thus administrative peccadilloes in welfare programmes often get more public exposure than do more expensive blunders by the military.

The story is much the same in Britain, only the Ministry of Defence no longer takes proportionately as large a chunk of the budget as in America. In 1973 to 1974, for instance, Defence received only £3·4 billion of the £18·6 billion spent by the national government. The armed forces stood at only 364,000 compared to a civil service of 701,000. Nonetheless, 173,000 civil servants still worked for the Ministry of Defence, and defence estimates still received special and separate treatment by Parliament. Moreover, MPs were even more ill-prepared than Congressmen to question requests of the military, let alone evaluate their performance.

Nor does the military sit back and wait for the legislature to debate its annual requests for appropriations. The military employs public-relations officers to promote its objectives; it adorns weapons systems with catchy salable labels; it carefully names its operations and exercises; and it cooperates fully with cinema and television producers who wish to dramatize its exploits. In short the military, like any other bureaucracy, attempts to build good will among the public at large. More than other agencies or departments, however, it has the ability to control the information that is released. Secrecy is central to national defence. No other government bureaucracy can make so bold a claim, and none has been so adept at releasing information favourable to its position at just the critical moments.

In sum the military presents the people's representatives not only with the problems of controlling a large bureaucracy, but of controlling one which has a *prima facie* claim to sequestering the very information which may be vital to evaluating how successfully it has performed its tasks.

4

The Corporations. Along with the growth of public bureaucracies has come the remarkable growth of huge private bureaucracies – the multinational corporations. Though legally constituted as 'persons', entities who owe and are owed, sue and are sued:

> ... they are not constrained by the prescribed three score years and ten. Second, corporations manage to avoid another frustrating human constraint, that of a single, explicit, unambiguous identity. A corporation can create offspring without limit, generate siblings as needed, even experience death and reincarnation.

> Though the corporation's attributes of unlimited life and multiple identity are revolutionary, its ability easily to acquire different nationalities for its offspring and siblings is even more so.[9]

Despite the revolutionary character of their growth and their impact upon the modern polity, liberal-democratic theory has been slow to take multinational – or even national – corporations into account. Corporations have been treated largely as any other private interest group in a pluralist democracy. Little has been made of their increasing control over the wealth, income, employment, and other resources of the polity. Even socialist critiques have not been revised much beyond the dreary shibboleths that corporations are bourgeois organizations that exploit the working classes, and that their capitalist owners ought to be (or will be) expropriated. That the National Coal Board gets on no better with its employees than does the Ford Motor Company, or that the Tennessee Valley Authority is as big a polluter as Consolidated Edison has not daunted those who favour nationalization. That workers are undeniably better off materially than they were when Marx and Engels developed their scientific theory of inevitability of social revolution has not brought about any fundamental revisions in traditional Marxian analyses concerning the fate of the bourgeois state.[10]

Yet the modern corporation is an entity without precedent in history. It is unique in the extent of its sales, assets, subsidiaries, product lines, market shares, and employee payrolls. It is also unique in its global reach and its supranational identity.

137

Table 4 Selected Corporations Compared with Selected Governmental Units (1975)

	Sales milliards (US billions)	Assets milliards (US billions)	Employees (1,000s)	Headquarters	World Rank
Industrial Corporations	$	$			(Sales)
Exxon	44·8	32·8	137	New York City	1
General Motors	35·7	21·6	681	Detroit, MI	2
Royal Dutch /Shell	32·1	28·3	161	London	3
British Petroleum	17·2	14·6	78	London	8
Unilever	15·0	6·9	321	London	10
International/ Tel./Telegraph	11·4	10·3	376	New York City	15
Commercial Banks	Deposits				(Deposits)
Bank of America	56·5	66·8	65	San Francisco, CA	1
Citicorp	44·7	57·8	46	New York City	2
Chase Manhattan	33·9	41·4	30	New York City	3
Barclay's	29·3	33·0	95	London	8
Utilities	Revenues				(Assets)
American Tel./Telegraph	28·9	80·1	377	New York City	1
Governments	Revenues	GDP	Government Employees	Total Civilian Employees (millions)	
USA (Federal)	281·0	1,516·0	2,897	84·8	
UK (Central)	23·6*	101·8*	1,596‡	24·7‡	
Sweden‡	29·0	55·9	812	4·0	

New York	25·6†	202	7·1
California	24·8†	273	7·8
Michigan	9·8†	143	3·3

SOURCES: Corporation data: *Fortune Magazine*, May, July and August 1976; Government Data: *Statistical Abstract of the United States*, 1976, Bureau of Census, Washington DC, 1976, tables 374, 409, 454, 591, 596; *Annual Abstract of Statistics*, 1975, Central Statistical Office, HMSO, London, 1975; table 352; *Britain 76, An Official Handbook*, HMSO, London, 1976, tables 26 and 27; *International Economic Indicators and Competitive Trends*, US Commerce Dept., Washington DC, Vol. II, No. 4, December 1976, p. 34; *OECD Economic Surveys: Sweden*, Organization of Economic Cooperation and Development, June 1975, tables A, D and basic statistics; *OECD Survey: Main Economic Indicators Organization for Economic Cooperation*, Paris, June 1976, p. 156; *State of New York Executive Budget*, Fiscal Year, 1 April 1976 to 31 March 1977; *Annual Report of State Controller of State of California*, Fiscal year ending 30 June 1975; *The Book of the States: 1976–77*, The Council of State Governments, Commercial Clearing House, Inc., Lexington KY, 1976; *The Swedish Budget: 1976/77*, Swedish Ministry of Finance, Stockholm, 1976, pp. 12–13.

* pounds (£) approximately $52·1 for government, $224·7 GDP.

† includes local government and federal transfer payments – state government revenue alone is approximately 40 per cent of this: NY 10·0 milliards; CA 10·2 milliards; MI 4·4 milliards

‡ 1974

The major multinational corporations are literally comparable to existing sovereign states. For instance, Exxon, the world's largest industrial firm, is incorporated in New York state (see table 4). According to American law, therefore, the firm is like any other 'person' in the state of New York. Although affected by federal law in its interstate and international commercial dealings, Exxon is ostensibly a taxpayer of the state of New York. But what an extraordinary taxpayer. This taxpayer happens to have more assets and more sales than its home state (including all its municipalities) has revenues, and it employs nearly as many people. Nor does it have a simple identity as do ordinary citizens, or a small 'mom and pop' grocery shop. Instead it has numerous subsidiary company identities which range from extracting, refining, manufacturing, distributing and marketing of various petroleum products (vertical integration) to parallel commercial ventures, involving other fuels, such as coal, uranium, and natural gas, and even to diversified ventures such as petrochemicals, insurance, and land development (horizontal integration).[11] As many of these subsidiaries are incorporated in other states and foreign countries, it is hard for the United States government, let alone the government of New York, to keep track of Exxon's operations for tax purposes. Keeping track of these operations is made doubly difficult by the fact that substantial portions of Exxon's expenditures involve intercompany transfers. And there is no guarantee that 'sales' between, say Exxon refining and Exxon pipeline shipping companies are not manipulated to gain each firm a more favourable tax position.[12]

Nor is Exxon subject to the uncertainties of the market place in the same manner as the small grocery shop. Exxon is a confirmed oligopolist. While Exxon itself controls less than 10 per cent of each segment of the American petroleum industry, the firm and a handful of sister corporations – Mobil, Gulf, BP, Shell, Texaco, Phillips, Atlantic-Richfield, Standard Oil of California, Standard Oil of Indiana, and National Iranian Oil – control better than 80 per cent of the world market in every aspect of petroleum processing from extraction and refining to distribution and retailing. These oligopolists are planners, not free enterprisers. They may compete with one another by advertising the quality of their products or the efficiencies of their service, but they rarely compete on the potentially deadly level of price. A gallon of Exxon petrol or heating oil can rarely be obtained at a price significantly different from a gallon of Gulf or Shell or BP. Each oligopolist is more concerned with maintaining its fair share of current and potential markets than with driving its rivals out of business in hopes of increasing its share.[13]

In fact oil companies cooperate with one another more often than they compete. By mutual understanding virtually every major oil field is divided among them, each to exploit its own sector, or several jointly to exploit a shared sector. The companies often share products with one another. The petrol at a motor plaza under the Exxon sign may well have been refined and delivered by another of the major companies. In Britain Shell and BP cooperate quite openly: abandoning all pretence of retail competition, they market their products together under a Shell–BP banner. Moreover the oil companies are now moving in tandem towards controlling other types of energy fuels, such as coal and uranium.[14]

The operations of multinational corporations are so large and far flung that despite their incorporation in one country, it makes sense to think of them as supranational entities, pursuing their own interests, whether or not those interests happen to coincide with the national interests of their home countries. Their methods of operation have become global in orientation, not biased in favour of one country or another.

The behaviour of the major oil companies during the Arab oil embargo in the autumn and winter of 1973 illustrates the extent to which multinationals have shed the shackles of national loyalty and identification. At the behest of the Saudi Arabian government Exxon, Texaco, Mobil, and Standard Oil of California – partners in the Arabian American Oil Company – turned over classified information concerning the country-by-country breakdown of the amounts of Mid East crude refined by their respective corporations to meet United States military needs. Of course Exxon warned the American Department of Defense of the impending turnover of the information. Generously it even allowed fifteen minutes for Pentagon officials to make their objections known. The other companies acted with a similar patriotic fervour.[15] To appreciate fully the implications of these actions for democratic theory, we must consider what would have occurred had the demand come from an ordinary member of Congress, a mere elected representative of the American people: it probably would have been refused by order of the Pentagon in the interests of national security.[16]

Yet the companies were not acting with any particular malice in this regard. They simply acted in their own sovereign interests. In this case it happened that what was good for Exxon was not good for the United States.

The point is that multinational corporations no longer consider their home countries' interests as primary. Investments are made where they will yield the best return, not where they will produce more jobs for the home country or help with its balance of payments. Large amounts of capital are kept liquid as a hedge not only against the home government's monetary policies, which might restrict investment, but also against the possibility of a devaluation, which might decrease corporate net worth. All this follows from the capitalist imperatives to seek growth and profits. The only difference from the past is that multinational corporations have grown so large that their privately motivated actions, gauged to exploit global-market conditions, often have severe impacts on the outcomes of public policies of nation states.

The magnitude of the largest multinational corporations is apparent not only when their sales, assets and employees are compared with features of governmental units, but also when they are compared with sales, assets, and employees of other manufacturing firms. Briefly stated, the top one-hundred manufacturing firms in Britain and the United States account for over half the manufacturing assets and sales. In America these same one-hundred manufacturers, together with the top three banks and ATT – a minuscule 0·005 per cent of all corporations – employ about 10 per cent of the civilian labour force. And in Britain the concentrations are equally impressive: five tobacco firms employ 98 per cent of tobacco workers; three oil refiners employ 71 percent; four sugar processors employ 96 per cent; and five computer manufacturers employ 79 per cent. The top 400 manufacturers account for about 20 per cent of all industrial employment. In sum the oligopoly of the oil industry represents the rule rather than the exception for major industries of Britain and the United States.[17]

Moreover, the trend in industrial development has been towards greater concentration ratios in Western societies, achieved largely by means of conglomerate mergers. Conglomerate mergers differ from ordinary vertical or horizontal mergers in that the merged companies may have no relation to one another's lines of business. Whereas Exxon and its subsidiaries engage mostly in business related directly or indirectly to extracting, processing and marketing fuel products, conglomerates like Unilever and ITT own dozens of unrelated businesses. Unilever doesn't just manufacture soaps and detergents; it is into food processing, building, auto dealing and distributing, and rubber plantations in Sierra Leone. ITT is not limited to businesses related to telephony and telegraphy; it owns publishing houses, insurance companies, rent-a-cars, bakeries, frozen-food companies, hotel chains, homebuilders, paper processors, and a community development corporation that is building its own new town. Needless to say governments find the activities of conglomerates even harder to monitor than those of ordinary multinationals. And in this situation the temptation for clever accountants to machinate the conglomerates' books for tax purposes must be very great.

While conglomerate mergers take place at home, foreign investment continues apace. By the early 70s American corporations had over $140 billion dollars capitalized in subsidiaries abroad, with estimated growth at 10 per cent per annum. British corporations had over $27 billion in foreign assets, and their investment too was growing though only at an annual rate of about 5 per cent. In both cases the profits from such investments were strong. American multinationals were realizing nearly 40 per cent of their net profits from foreign operations and investments. Meanwhile, private ventures abroad were so profitable to British industries that the profits, dividends, interest, and payments for services – the invisible transactions – offset otherwise negative trade balances in 1971 and 1972.[18]

The multinationals have been generally supported in all these expansive operations by the large commercial banks. As in manufacturing, the concentration of assets controlled by the largest banks has been increasing. And so too, have their foreign deposits. Although there are approximately 14,000 banks in the United States, the top one-hundred hold over half of all deposits. And with regard to foreign deposits the concentration is even greater: the top twenty control nearly all of them. In the United Kingdom the banking concentration is greater yet. Six commercial banking groups control 36 per cent of all deposits in the banking system. And much of the rest is tied up not in ordinary deposits or current accounts, but in the discount market, which, in conjunction with the Bank of England, performs many of the functions of the American Federal Reserve System.

In 1972 the six commercial groups held £18,170 million in deposits, while the National Savings Bonds, postal savings, National Savings Bank deposits, and trustee savings – amounted to little over £10,000 million. Beyond this the six commercial banking groups account for virtually all the overseas banking operations either directly or through specially formed subsidiaries.[19]

Cooperation between large firms and the major banks is facilitated through interlocking directorates, prominent officers of major banks serving on the boards of the multinational corporations. In 1968, for instance, the House Committee on Banking and Currency discovered that the top forty-nine banks in America were linked with 286 of the largest 500 corporations through 768 interlocking directorates. These same banks controlled at least 5 per cent of the voting stock in 147 of these corporations.[20] Similar links between the directorates of thirty-one of the top forty industrial firms and twenty-seven prominent financial institutions were found in Britain. And in comparison to the United States the members of these elite directorates were more likely to have had both similar education training – attendance at public schools and Oxbridge colleges – and similar social ties – and membership in one or more of the nine most prestigious London clubs.[21]

Global corporations deliberately participate in politics in a number of ways. As does the military, the major corporations invest heavily in building favourable public images in hopes that the good will obtained can be translated into political support when needed. Our popular culture abounds with corporate symbols and slogans. Tate and Lyle's Mr Cube, veteran cartoon character of the Sugar Industry's anti-nationalization campaign against the Attlee Government, still appears from time to time on packaging and advertisements to win friends for sugar processors and for private enterprise in general. Robertson's golliwogs, available for a pittance plus a few jam-jar labels, have warmed many young hearts to the British food industry – at least until recently, when the dolls began to gather undertones of racial disrespect. Mobil's pedantic advertisements about the energy crisis are designed not so much to sell petroleum products as to sell the idea of Mobil's benevolent concern for energy matters and to provide the public with arguments for less regulation of the energy industry. US Steel's 'We're involved' advertisements hardly get the public to buy tungsten steel for jet engines or wide gauge seamless pipe for pumping oil, but they should bring some sympathy when the company claims that the Federal Government has set unreasonably burdensome regulations for its coking operations. How well corporations have succeeded in their public campaign is perhaps best attested to by the large numbers of citizens who sport T-shirts emblazoned with corporate products or emblems.[22]

More directly, corporate spokesmen lobby legislative and bureaucratic decision-makers; corporate officers serve on government advisory committees and regulatory commissions; and corporate boards channel funds – by legal and illegal means – into the coffers of political parties and candidates. While corporations have not been entirely successful in convincing governments to adopt their policy preferences, critics like Barnett and Müller, as quoted at the head of this chapter, judge that their influence nonetheless has been far too great, especially in the area of economic planning. More importantly, there seems to be little recognition of the potential if not actual power of corporations to manipulate public policy. Public agencies remain largely dependent upon corporate sources for much needed information about natural resources, technological capabilities and costs. No one save the oil companies, for instance, has the means to estimate the world reserves of oil and natural gas. And none but these same companies can give any true estimate of the rate at which the aforementioned reserves are being depleted. Such control of critical information in a few private hands does not augur well for the democratic *bona fides* of governmental decision-making.

Finally, the global nature of the impact of the activities of multinational corporations have not been fully appreciated by governments. The growth of international business has far outstripped the abilities of national governments and international agencies to monitor their transactions. Indeed it is questionable whether the current arrangements of political institutions are sufficient to enable governments to monitor the activities of multinational corporations – much less to control them – even if the governments so desired:

It is not only international agencies that need data on international business. How can any country develop an effective policy to influence exports and foreign exchange earnings without taking into account the decisions of international business firms into their strategies? Yet policy makers are only beginning to recognize the important role being played by international business. If they want to include international business in their considerations, they will quickly discover that they have not been collecting the necessary factual information.[23]

Clearly, any theory of democracy that does not take account of the activities of multinational corporations will not provide much guidance for the conduct of politics today. The activities of corporations in the modern polity are too important to ignore.

5

Environmental factors. In the preceding sections we have argued that orthodox statements of liberal democracy do not take sufficient account of powerful new actors in the polity, namely, the government bureaucracy, the military, and the multinational corporations. The implication of this argument is that great concentrations of power in the hands of the unelected greatly increase the probability that public-policy decisions will be arrived at by means other than democratic. These elites – the technological experts and the very wealthy – possess the means to manipulate the ordinary citizen to such an extent as to render his political participation nothing more than a sham.

Indeed the case has been made that these elites have already assured the success of most of their political objectives, for the rules of governing have been written in their favour. Despite the supposedly redistributive effects of tax laws, for instance, the fact remains that neither income nor wealth has been redistributed to any substantial degree since the Second World War. In both Britain and the United States the top 5 per cent receive more total income than the bottom 30 per cent, even after taxes. Wealth – stocks, bonds, real estate and the like – is even more concentrated; and taxes on wealth are less redistributive than those on income.[24] These great concentrations of income and wealth are employed to maintain the privileged positions of the elites. Millions are spent on public relations to enhance the images of the elites; additional millions are spent gathering and supplying mass media and government decision-makers with information supportive of policies the elites favour. And even when government seeks independent sources of information, it is often forced nonetheless to fall back upon the expertise of the elites, either directly, through hearing advice and testimony from corporate or military personnel or indirectly through employment of said personnel seconded from corporate payrolls or the military to serve on government advisory and regulatory boards. And in those rare circumstances when members of the elite are caught transgressing the law, government charitably turns the other cheek. When General Electric and Westinghouse were found guilty of pricefixing in the early 1960s the Internal Revenue Service generously allowed them to deduct their fines from their taxes as necessary business expenses. Less than a year after their convictions for illegal contributions of corporate funds to President Nixon's 1972 re-election campaign, fifteen of twenty-one executives were back on the job or drawing healthy pensions from their corporations. None was in gaol; one has his case still on appeal. Crime in the executive suites – clean, white-collar crime – is treated more gently than crime in the streets.[25]

Pluralists of course reject the contention that a narrow set of elites control public policy. They point out that corporate and military leaders often cannot agree among themselves about policy, let alone convince bureaucrats and legislators to follow their lead. They see a more competitive relationship among a diversity of elites – a system of contervailing powers that includes not just the military, bureaucratic and corporate elites, but unions, cause groups, and other voluntary associations.[26] And as long as these groups remain accessible to citizens who desire to participate, or at least responsive to the ideas of citizens who are not members, then pluralists are satisfied that democratic politics prevail.[27]

For our present purposes we need not reevaluate the relative merits of the elitist versus pluralist interpretations of the politics of Western industrial states. Even if we grant the most optimistic view of the good intentions of the elites; even if we assume that the elite decision-making structures are easily accessible to the plea of any citizen; even if we go so far as to presume that like our mythical Good Citizen Brown every political leader takes into account the interest of the community as well as his own; the polity described – however liberal and democratic – may not be viable.

The problem is that conventional descriptions of liberal democracy, which emphasize the maximization of individual self-development, self-expression, and self-aggrandizement, reflect a series of unsupportable assumptions about the extent of nature's bounty and the limits of human technology's ability to exploit it. Almost from the beginning, in the works of Hobbes and Locke down through those of Smith, Bentham and Spencer, liberalism has been associated with an economic system based upon the unfettered ability of individuals to accumulate privately both consumer and capital goods. The impact of socialist thought upon liberalism was to democratize it. Although they did not accept the socialist idea of collectivizing scarce capital goods, liberals did come to accept the contention that the productive capacity of the new industrial technology held promise of an abundance

148

of consumer goods for all. Not only could modern industry provide the necessities of food, clothing, and shelter, but it could also provide sufficient wherewithal to give individual citizens the luxury of choosing from a wide variety of non-necessities, items heretofore reserved only for the consumption of the well-to-do. And once the average citizen achieved a modest level of affluence it naturally followed that like his Athenian forebears he would develop the interest and the ability to take an active part in the affairs of state. To encourage this development, educational opportunities were expanded and the last major barriers to political participation – property and sexual qualifications – were removed.

The tenets of twentieth-century liberal democracy, then, were based optimistically upon a faith in the unlimited capacities of modern technology to fulfil the wants of a consumer-oriented society. Though class-distinctions might remain, they supposedly would not be invidious. The attainment of high status would be achieved largely through each individual's own efforts, not through the accident of birth. Thus an aristocracy of talent, not absolute equality, would be the mark of liberal-democratic polity.

And, in truth, the economies of liberal-democratic politics have been phenomenally successful. Despite two world wars; despite the great depression and lesser economic downturns; despite challenges of the fascist right and the communist left; the citizens of Western Europe, North America, Australia, and (since the Second World War) Japan have enjoyed unprecedented economic growth and prosperity. The very success of these economies has been displayed as if it constituted proof of the prowess of liberal-democratic regimes, and these regimes have very generously described the workings of their political and economic institutions as models for less fortunate nations to emulate. It is only recently that citizens of these industrially successful nations have begun to sense that something has gone awry:

Cities are becoming uninhabitable just when almost everyone is compelled to live in them; nature is polluted and destroyed just when people feel a growing need to enjoy it; all modes of travel are intolerable just when journeys are increasing in number and length; old age takes on the proportions of a curse just when the ratio of the old to the young is rising; the grip of bigness is tightening just when everyone is acquiring the material and cultural means to enhance his own individuality; and so on.[28]

The consequences of the false assumptions underlying the economies of the advanced industrial nations have become manifest. The biosphere itself, ravished by men's greedy pursuit of material self-aggrandizement, seems on the verge of ecological disaster. It suddenly became apparent that there are too few acres of land, even too few fish in the sea, to provide the world population with a diet of the sort consumed by citizens of liberal-democratic nations. It has also become clear that there are neither the mineral resources nor the fossil fuels to support in the developing nations the sort of industrial growth the advanced nations have experienced. Indeed, without some drastic changes in the patterns and the rates of consumption of these resources in industrially advanced nations, even their current levels of output cannot be sustained. And to top things off, regardless of availability of raw materials, the levels of environmental pollution caused by current rates of production threaten to make the earth uninhabitable.

Whilst we do not have to accept all the grim conclusions of Malthusian economics regarding world food resources, the populations of poorer nations plainly cannot be sustained through adoption of the 'superior' dietary habits of the richer industrial nations. In fact if the masses of most poorer countries are to receive proper nourishment – surely a prerequisite for viable democratic governance – then wasteful Western dietary habits, which convert large amounts of cheap protein in grain into small amounts of expensive protein in meat, must be abandoned. Even preferences of citizens of industrial countries for protein from certain species of fish, such as cod, now in short supply, must be curbed. There is a certain irony here. In order to promote democracy abroad – perhaps even to preserve it at home – liberal democrats will have to give up certain accustomed rights – at the very least, the right to consume whatever foods they can afford.

And what if we succeed in husbanding world agricultural resources efficiently enough to nourish today's population? We still must institute effective limitations on population growth; otherwise world famine is our fate. Also, if voluntary programmes of birth control are not successful, we face a time when even the right to bear children will be significantly curtailed.[29]

Food and population problems aside, we still face increasingly acute shortages of raw materials and energy resources that have gone into producing the goods that characterize the vaunted standards of living of liberal democracies. One does not have to assume the mantle of a doomsday prophet to calculate that present levels of consumption of various minerals – aluminium, copper, lead, tin, and zinc – and fossil fuels (other than coal) will not be sustainable much beyond the turn of the century, if that long.[30] And how much more rapidly will these natural resources deplete, if non-industrial nations attempt to replicate the industrial economies of liberal-democratic nations? Once more an irony: in order to promote and perpetuate liberal democracy, citizens of liberal-democratic nations will have to surrender their accustomed right to consume unlimited amounts of natural resources.

Finally, our problems have come full circle: from the necessity of removing dung from the streets of medieval towns we have advanced to the necessity of removing industrial waste from the air and oceans. Only now the problem is worse. Instead of organic materials which eventually decompose naturally, we find inorganic pollutants: insecticides which accumulate in the food chain; plastics which never break down; radioactive wastes with half-lives of thousands of years. Thanks to the industrial advances of liberal-democratic nations and their non-liberal industrial competitors, humanity faces the real possibility of extinction, the by-products of industrial affluence threatening to render the planet uninhabitable. As a matter of survival the freedom to consume so cherished by liberal democrats once again will have to be curtailed; and curbs on pollution will necessitate curbs on the choices of products available to consumers.

Here we are not talking about making some mild adjustments in response to temporary problems, but about taking unwonted draconian measures to assure our very survival – measures of such severity that critics like Heilbroner fear that democratic governments will not be able to undertake them.[31] Why is this so?

In a word 'more' has been the motto of liberal-democratic nations. Democratization of their governmental institutions has been largely painless because it has entailed no accompanying redistribution – democratization, if you will – of the wealth and income of the privileged. The lot of the lower classes has improved only because the whole economic pie has grown, not because they have gained a relatively greater slice. The bottom 20 per cent are better off getting 5 per cent of a billion (US trillion) dollar pie than they were getting 5 per cent of a milliard (US billion) dollar one. But their proportion of that pie has not increased.

What happens now that the economic pie must cease to grow? It is questionable whether the necessary adjustments can be accomplished democratically. Will the elite be willing to share a greater portion of their wealth with the masses? More broadly, will the richer nations be willing to share a portion of their affluence with the poorer? [32] There is no dodging these questions; present and projected levels of technology will not save us from the problems they pose. The pat answers – that fission reactors will resolve the energy crisis; that North Sea and Alaskan oil will keep our cars on the road; that, as always, new deposits of minerals will be found – are mistaken. A period of severe adjustment in our economic and political institutions lies ahead. What is to be done?

First, we must abandon the myth of perpetual economic growth. We shall abandon it deliberately or else circumstances will force us to abandon it willy-nilly, for present resources and technologies simply will not sustain it. Secondly, we must adopt a new system of bookkeeping for measuring economic progress. Instead of improved standards of living as measured by gross national products, we need improved quality of life as measured by lower levels of air and water pollution, fewer instances of preventable disease, fewer outbreaks of social strife, more enjoyment of recreation and the arts. Thirdly, we need to seek new technologies emphasizing permanence and recycling. Planned obsolescence, wanton waste of natural resources, can no longer be tolerated. Finally, we need to develop new types of energy resources independent of fossil fuels: technologies utilizing solar, geothermal, wind, and nuclear-fusion energy must be advanced.[33]

Unfortunately all of the above mentioned changes go against the dominant economic values of liberal democracies. The primary objectives of capitalist corporations are growth and profits, and the political leaders who have gainsaid these objectives are few. Moreover, the accounting systems of both government and business deal only in readily quantifiable items one can buy or sell. The value of an unscarred mountainside standing against a clear blue sky, clear streams running down its gullies, is simply ignored. If the cheapest, most profit-efficient method of obtaining a mineral is to strip away the mountainside, befouling the air and the water, then stripped it will be. The cost of befouling the air and water – even the cost of depleting the mineral – will never show up on the books. Permanence? The incentives are all for maintaining short-term profit and growth. Permanence suggests people might stop consuming at ever increasing rates, that the market might be glutted with unbought items. Are we not told how important it is for us to purchase our annual quota of new cars? How else will we sell enough steel and enough rubber tyres? It seems that the purpose of acquiring an automobile is to provide jobs for workers and profits for manufacturers in the automobile, steel and rubber industries. It seems that it has little to do with acquiring transportation. Finally, the development of new types of energy resources is uneconomic, at least for the present. There are far bigger profits to be realized by taking advantage of recurring shortages of fossil fuels. British and American oil company profits soared during the winter of 1973; American natural-gas company profits did the same in the winter of 1976. Until these fossil fuels are nearly exhausted – a determination which only the companies have the information to make – it pays to hold off developing new and possibly competitive energy resources.

This resistance to the sorts of necessary economic adjustments discussed above is hardly out of malice. It may stem from the best of capitalistic intentions. After all, economic growth is the American way: bigger and better. The American economy produced the highest standard of living in the world and other liberal democracies in turn emulated its success. Why should the economic growth to which liberal democracies have grown accustomed be abandoned? Sacrificing current profits for pollution control, short-term economic efficiency for long-term energy efficiency, cheap short-lived products for more expensive long-lived ones, makes little sense given the current accounting systems. It means, at the very least, a painful reorientation and (possibly) retooling, likely to cut into profit over several fiscal years. And less profit means less expansion which means fewer jobs. Fewer jobs are followed by less pay, less purchasing power, recession, depression, or worse. In order to maintain their citizens' standards of living, the economies of liberal democracies, like Alice, must run very fast.

6

The Survival of Democracy. The idea of liberal democracy has a long and honourable history. Embodied in Anglo-American political institutions, devoted to maintaining open a wide range of alternative opportunities for individual self-expression and development, it has contributed to the advancement of man as a civilized rational being. It has proved a flexible doctrine, able to adjust to criticisms, such as its relative lack of concern for the rights of the community as opposed to those of the individual, its initial unsubstantiated certainty that natural rights could be discovered by reason alone, and its nineteenth-century association with *laissez-faire* economics. And in the twentieth century it has withstood the challenges of both communism and fascism, and it has resisted allegations that ordinary citizens are not rational enough to participate in democratic politics.

In the latter half of the twentieth century, however, several developments have culminated in challenges of a sort which had not previously been given thorough consideration by liberal democrats. The public bureaucracy has threatened to disempower the legislature, the central political institution of liberal democracy. The military has used its increased resources, particularly its control over sensitive and highly technical information, to attempt to manipulate public policy in its own favour. And the large private corporations have assumed such a great concentration of wealth, income and employment opportunities that their ostensibly private decisions, concerning economic investment and planning, have made a greater impact than many public-policy decisions. Finally, shortages of natural resources, coupled with the dangers of environmental pollution, threaten to destroy the liberal-democratic dream of achieving through economic growth a modicum of prosperity for all without the need to force redistribution of wealth from rich to poor within countries or from rich countries to poor ones.

If democracy is to survive, it would seem that some serious revisions to liberal-democratic theory are in order. Eighteenth- and nineteenth-century political institutions must be reformed and upgraded to deal with twentieth-century problems. At the same time citizens must be encouraged to develop their own rational faculties, not excused from all but periodic consideration of politics at election times. The challenge is formidable. We must build a theory of viable democracy, one that preserves traditional concerns for individual self-development through political participation, but one that also takes into account the realities of the bureaucracy, the military and corporate establishment, and the environment.

In the next chapter we make an attempt to build such a theory.

7 · Viable Democracy

Contemporary industrial civilization demonstrates that it has reached the stage at which 'the free society' can no longer be adequately defined in the traditional terms of economic, political, and intellectual liberties, not because these liberties have become insignificant, but because they are too significant to be confined within the traditional forms. New modes of realization are needed, corresponding to the new capabilities of society.

Herbert Marcuse, *One-Dimensional Man*, Merlin Press, 1964.

I

The task before us is to present our promised statement of a theory of liberal democracy for the last decades of the twentieth century. The arguments of the preceding chapters have laid out the requirements of this task.

To begin with, our theory must provide for substantially equal opportunity for meaningful participation in politics by all adult citizens. By 'meaningful participation in politics' we mean participation that demonstrably has more than a negligible probability of affecting the outcomes of the events towards which that participation is directed.[1] Voting in an election in which all the candidates have been screened and certified by the governing elite, for instance, does not constitute meaningful participation. Neither does presentation of evidence at a public hearing in which the most relevant data have been classified by the government or remain the exclusive property of a technological elite.

Secondly, our theory must be liberal. It should provide ample opportunity for diverse life styles and for individual self-development. While individual liberties must be limited by both the necessity of accommodating one's fellow citizens in an orderly fashion, and the necessity of accommodating one's life style to the limitations of the polity's natural resources, liberal democracies should be distinguishable nonetheless from polities that are not liberal. One test of this liberalism is the ability of ordinary citizens to place alternatives they favour into the political arena for public consideration. If the agenda of politics is set only by the political elite, liberalism probably is lacking.

Thirdly, the theory should posit a set of political institutions capable of dealing with twentieth-century problems in democratic fashion. The people or their elected representatives should have sufficient means to control the government bureaucracy, the military and the large corporations. The potential for control must extend not only to traditional areas of government regulations, such as protection of civil rights or enforcement of contracts, but also to the control of the exploitation of natural resources and the pollution of the natural environment. Without such capabilities *de facto* political control will devolve upon unelected elites.

Finally, our theory should demand a level and quality of participation commensurate with citizens' willingness and ability to particpate. In short, the demands we make of citizens should be realistic in terms of the findings of political science concerning citizens' political behaviour.

This is a tall order, but not an impossible one. Once we cease to limit our thought to how the traditional political institutions of liberal democracies currently function, the task becomes a good deal easier. What we shall propose makes heavy use of new developments in the field of communications, developments which representative political institutions, legislatures in particular, have largely ignored. As it turns out these developments have the potential of providing citizens and their elected representatives with unaccustomed access to the data necessary to effect far greater control of governmental decision-making.

We shall not be coy in presenting our theory. Rather than reserving it for the climax, having rejected all others, we shall present it forthwith in the next two sections. Only then shall we defend it against alternatives of a more traditional nature. Finally, we shall assess the prospects of implementing the changes our theory recommends.

2

A Theory of Viable Democracy, Part One: An Information Network. As we have suggested from the beginning, modern democratic regimes need to enhance the capability of their political institutions to deal with twentieth-centry political problems. Modern technology has simply outdistanced the current capabilities of democratic political institutions, especially the elected legislatures, to deal with it. As a result, bureaucratic elites, both public and private, have exerted increasing amounts of influence and control over public policy. Our theory of viable democracy seeks to redress this imbalance by employing modern data-processing technology in service of the ordinary citizens in order to enhance their governing capabilities and those of their elected representatives. The key element of our theory is the distribution of information. We contend that citizens and their representatives need cheaper, more efficient access to relevant information about political problems and events of concern to them. They don't need more information per se; they need more *relevant* information, well-organized and easily accessible. And once they have said information, they need cheap and efficient ways to communicate with one another and with the appropriate political decision-makers.

It there really a need for more relevant information? After all, as we have seen, citizens are typically – and quite sensibly – concerned about only a few political problems and events, not the whole spectrum of politics. (Who, but a select, highly motivated minority, could find time to consider more than a few major issues in an intelligent manner?) Yet citizens typically know a good deal about those relatively few problems with which they have great concern. Furthermore, as the subsets of problems and events with which any two groups of citizens concern themselves are unlikely to be the same, it is probable that the concerns of different but reasonably well-informed groups of citizens taken together do indeed cover the whole spectrum of politics.[2] Thus more information, regardless of its relevance, might seem redundant.

We contend, however, that relevant information about political problems is often lacking. Under present conditions ordinary citizens depend largely upon mass media for information about politics. To be sure, some belong to specialized groups or subscribe to specialized services that augment their information about specific areas of interest, but most still rely on the media to call their attention to a problem.[3]

An immediate difficulty here is that mass media are, as their descriptive adjective implies, for the masses. In order to satisfy the diversity of interests of their audience they tend to cover a broad range of topics and to avoid presentation of detailed information, except on those few subjects which their editors judge as having great popular appeal. Citizens who read about a particular aspect of politics in the *Economist* or *Time* are unlikely to acquire much more information about it by turning to *Newsweek* or the Sunday papers. They will acquire even less from listening to radio or television. To get better information they will have to turn to specialized private or governmental publications housed in large library collections or available directly from the original sources.

A second difficulty is that the mass media themselves devote rather limited resources to gathering political information. News of political events must vie for media attention with news of crime, sports, business, and human interest. Local and regional newspapers, television, and radio stations normally provide coverage in depth of only the most dramatic local political events. And for coverage of events outside their territory, these local media rely upon a limited number of new services, such as Reuters, United Press International, the Associated Press, or the big radio–television network news operations. But these news services in turn devote only a portion of their reporters' time and energy to coverage of political events. In addition, investigative reporting of politics, as compared with straight coverage of political events, receives little funding. Government itself devotes more money and manpower to gathering and disseminating political information than do major newspapers, news agencies, radio and television networks.[4] And although the actual resources major corporations devote to politics are not a matter of public record, it is safe to wager that they also devote more resources to their own areas of political interest than do the mass media. In fact government and corporate spokespersons are often the primary source of news stories covered by the media. Upon closer examination, then, the mass media emerge as less powerful and less independent than they would seem at first blush.

But what of those citizens who persevere in their attempts to gather information? Will not perusal of specialized publications, obtainable in libraries or from private sources, provide sufficient relevant information? Only sometimes – for it happens that the relevant documents often originate from those very government or corporate sources that the citizen wishes to check upon. Take the energy problem, for example. The only official estimates of reserves of fossil fuels in the United States are derived from those of the energy industry, precisely the people upon whose credibility the citizen may be seeking information to check. And even when the sources are seemingly independent scholars, it may turn out that the documentation and interpretations were inspired by government or corporate elites through judicious release of portions of otherwise unavailable material. By this means, for example, the CIA and USIA inspired the publication and distribution of at least sixteen books in the mid sixties, published by such reputable firms as Frederick A. Praeger and the MIT Press, but bearing no trace of government imprimatur.[5] Even if we ignore problems of the reliability of the information sources, it is still unrealistic to expect more than a few of the minority of citizens ordinarily interested in a given political problem to take the time and trouble to visit the library, or otherwise to seek out specialized information on that problem.

Fortunately, much of this dependency on second-hand information from the media or from documents of questionable authenticity can be overcome. With the power of modern communications-technology, it is feasible to facilitate direct access for citizens or their representatives to most of the documentary information which forms the basis of the media reports. The means of accomplishing this is extensive public access to computer-based information systems, systems already in widespread use among civilian and military bureaucracies, big corporations, universities, hospitals, and other large-scale organizations.

The equipment for implementing such access is already at hand. Basically all that is required is a computer console resembling a typewriter and costing not much more. Such a console can be connected to a computer network through existing telephone lines or, more practically, through cable-television lines, which will be commonplace in millions of homes in the next decade.[6] The ordinary television screen can be used to display data or, for some additional cost, hard copies can be typed out or printed.

Such a computer-based network can be operated in interactive mode. That is, instead of communications flowing only one way, the citizen users can converse with the system, inquire about information available, delve as superficially or as deeply into subjects as they desire. Moreover, the network can also operate as a decentralized communication system. As a consequence, users need not limit themselves to inquiries only. Any user of a properly programmed network should be able to send messages to any other user (or classes of users). In practical terms this means that a citizen could easily send a message to any of his representatives, indicating his opinions about some subjects, his ability or desire to present new information, or any other suggestions he thought appropriate. And members of organized groups could easily communicate with one another and exchange information.[7]

It must be emphasized, however, that we are not describing an 'instant democracy', a political system where policy questions are posed via the computer and resolved by daily plebiscites.[8] Most citizens, as we have seen, are not interested in most political issues; and it would be unreasonable to demand that they pay attention to every question of public policy. We aim instead to provide equal opportunity for every citizen to gather information and express himself about those questions which interest him. While no artificial barriers will preclude any citizen from becoming involved in every given policy question, limitations of time and energy, not to mention diversity of personal interests, will almost certainly lead different groups of citizens to become concerned about different issues. In all likelihood a broader (albeit still elite) type of political participation will develop – a democratic form of pluralism.

Of course technological feasibility is not the same as implementation. A number of questions must be faced regarding implementation of such a network. What information goes on the network? What restrictions, if any, should limit access to that information? How should citizen users be protected from unscrupulous or abusive use of the information on the network, especially that information which touches directly on the citizens' private lives? Who programmes the network? How are maintenance and usage of the network to be paid for? And finally, what other new features are needed besides the network in order to facilitate democratic governance?

To begin with all computerized records of government agencies, both civilian and military, should be made accessible. In addition, indices to major government documents should also be included. Finally, information on current legislative proposals, administrative regulations, and court cases should be added.

There should be no objections in principle to placing the information listed above on the network. Liberal democracy is founded upon a belief in the capabilities of the average citizen to decide fundamental questions of public policy. But if the citizen is to decide rationally he, or his elected representative, needs access to relevant data held by all agencies of government. In principle citizens or their representatives already have such access in any country claiming to be a liberal democracy. The network in this case only serves to facilitate that access.

Of course the matter is not as simple as it seems in this description. Some governmental data are sensitive. For reasons of national security or for reasons of private rights the general release of such data could prove injurious to the polity or to numerous private citizens. Later in our discussion, therefore, serious consideration must be given to the question of restricting general access to some of these data.[9] But first, let us continue specifying the sort of data to be included on the information network.

Included also should be the computerized records of those groups, ostensibly in the private sector, whose actions, as we have observed, substantially affect the outcomes of public policies. These are the major manufacturing corporations, utilities and banks. Where we argued before that no modern democratic government can function successfully without taking into account the policies and decisions of these powerful political actors, we now suggest that governments can make no proper assessment of these policies and decisions without access to the data upon which they are based. It is patently absurd to pretend that the 'private' computerized records of these huge organizations deserve the same protection from public scrutiny as do mama's love letters, papa's personal diary, or Farmer Jones's private library. The impact of the organizational decisions derived from these records is so great that by and large the records themselves should be treated as public in the same manner that the records of governmental agencies are public. This means of course that similar restrictions to open access to sensitive data should also apply.

Finally we want to include the computerized records of other businesses, industries and associations currently subject to regulation by public boards or commissions. Here we are including a broad range of organizations. Some of them are relatively small, but each shares the feature that the people's representatives have already decided that they are of sufficient importance to the public to be subjected to special regulations. As the sensitivity of many records in this area, such as medical treatment in hospitals, disciplinary actions in schools, or amounts of income from private pensions, is obvious, there must accordingly be more restriction of access to these data than there is to data regarding governmental agencies, major corporations, banks and utilities.

Before turning to a consideration of these restrictions, some prefatory remarks about desired technological features of the information network are necessary. First, the system must be simple to use, designed for ordinary citizens with little or no background in computing. Secondly, it must be cheap to use. Thirdly, it must be capable of expansion without significant alteration in the manner in which data are accessed. Finally, it must be self-documenting, programmed to provide users with instructions on how to employ its capabilities. Unfortunately, although all these features are technologically possible, to our knowledge no large-scale computer network in operation incorporates all of them.[10] Nonetheless we shall proceed with our discussion with the expectation that these technological problems will be solved, concentrating instead upon the politically relevant problems of instituting the network.

Let us begin by stating two principles that should govern access to relevant information in a viable democracy: 1) all computerized files of every appropriately designated organization, whether public or private, must be accessible through the information network; 2) while restricting the access of the general public to some sensitive data will be necessary, in no case should any such computerized information be excluded from the purview of the elected members of the central legislature. These principles are hardly self-evident. They require some defence.

It may be immediately objected, for instance, that the first principle includes too much. Is there not a good deal of information that *prima facie* is none of the public's business? How about military secrets; investigative records; trade secrets and manufacturing formulae; private lists of inventories, profits, and clientele; medical records; information about credit and insurance?[11] The answer of course is that some of these data, indeed, are not the public's business. But the problems of protecting their confidentiality are not insurmountable. For one thing some sensitive information can be protected simply by not computerizing it. Secret military orders, manufacturing formulae, and confidential lists would seem to fall in this category. Other data may be shielded from public access in accordance with general principles laid down by legislation or through exclusions granted by special legislation. In any case the burden of demonstrating the necessity of restricting access to data should fall upon those who wish to restrict it. They must convince the people's elected representatives (or their designates) that such restriction is required. Otherwise citizens will find themselves facing the same problems of inaccessibility of proprietary information that they presently face.

Now it may also be objected that the second principle entrusts the legislators with too much sensitive information. After all, history has shown that some legislators are prone to exploit such information for their own sensational purposes. Will not the proposed information network simply smooth the way for demagogues like Enoch Powell or the late Joseph McCarthy to work their will?

Some unscrupulous legislators will undoubtedly attempt to exploit their privileged access to information for private advantage, as they have done in the past. But it is important to keep in mind that this is a theory of liberal democracy we are expounding. Its fundamental premise is the reasonableness of the citizenry. If all legislators have access to the same information, then the demagogues at least will have no special advantage. Liberal democrats must have faith that the large majority of legislators and other governmental officials will act to check the demagogues by exposing their false or distorted claims to public scrutiny, and that, faced with such evidence, a reasonable citizenry will have the good sense to reject their demagogic appeals. Beyond this it is reasonable for liberal democrats to expect that at the next election citizens will decide to oust the demagogues and to return responsible legislators in their place.

At any rate consider the alternatives. To whom shall such sensitive information be entrusted, if not to the citizens' representatives? Shall the information be left in the hands of the unelected, the bureaucrats and technological elites? What assurances do we have that these people will act in the public interest more often than will the legislators? At least the legislators must answer directly to the citizenry; the others need not.

Our discussion of the principles for determining access to the data on the proposed information network, however, has only touched upon the complex problem of protecting the ordinary citizen from unscrupulous use of files of information about himself. The problem arises from our attempt to incorporate both democracy and liberalism into our theory of viable democracy. These two concepts, as we have seen, are by no means identical.[12] We say that in a modern mass society, democracy, defined as equal opportunity to participate in politics, can only be achieved if each citizen has substantially equal access to politically relevant information. The proposed information network provides a means for such access, but in doing so it also poses a danger to liberal government. The object of liberal government, we recall, is to maintain open the fullest possible range of options and values for the individual in order to facilitate his personal development and self-expression. In a viable democracy a number of private decisions an individual makes – to buy stocks, bonds, or insurance; to write an overdraft or to obtain a loan; to join a company pension plan; to receive treatment in hospital – all become recorded on the public-information network. Why? Because the policies and actions of the agencies or organizations involved with these decisions – stock markets, insurance companies, banks and other lending agencies, pension plans, and hospitals – have been deemed important enough to become subject to public regulation or control. The expectation that one's everyday choices as a private citizen may be recorded for public distribution will often inhibit those choices and thereby inhibit the personal development and self-expression of each citizen.

How can this problem be solved? In fact it cannot. Short of forbidding computerization of any personal information about individuals, there is no absolute guarantee that some clever programmer with access to the relevant computer system will not be able to penetrate even the most elaborate schemes for file protection. And even though networking of data exacerbates this problem by facilitating access to each computerized file, it nonetheless confers enormous benefits by increasing the information capacities of citizens and their elected representatives. Forbidding computerization would make sensitive records susceptible to access by fewer unauthorized individuals, but it would not prevent abuses by unscrupulous members of the organizations or agencies in possession of the files. Moreover, it would be harder to trace those who made unauthorized use of the files, for unlike a properly monitored computer file, no record could be made automatically of those who accessed the information.

Our contention is that although the problem of unauthorized access to and abuse of personal data files cannot be eliminated, it can be substantially alleviated if the appropriate measures are taken. In fact the dangers of abuse may actually turn out to be less than those which exist currently, for at the moment computerized personal files remain the private preserve of selected government agencies and private organizations. Let us look at some of these measures designed to protect the citizen from abusive use of his personal files.

First and foremost every citizen must by right have full access to any files about himself. Not only must each citizen have this access, but he must also have the right to challenge and have corrected any information which cannot be documented as accurate. Nor should it be difficult for the citizen to exercise his right to access his personal file. Annually, along with his tax forms, each citizen should receive a listing of all his personal files on the information network, together with instructions on how to access them for examination. At this time the citizen should also receive a listing of all users – (presumably) authorized citizens and organizations – who accessed any of his records over the past year. (The citizen of course should be able to receive an update of these annual listings at other times during the year via the information network.) Finally the law should provide for strict enforcement of rules for access, buttressed by penalties for unauthorized access to or abuse of data on personal information files. The penalties should be similar to those currently on the books for unwarranted invasion of privacy.

To go into any more detailed discussion of specific rules for access to sensitive data would add little of substance at this stage. Suffice it to say that the rules for access must balance the citizens' need for politically relevant information against their need for privacy in personal affairs. Different polities will undoubtedly arrive at different balances between these needs. The important point is that both be explicitly recognized and taken into account in developing rules of access to sensitive data as appropriate to the circumstances of the polity.

Even after the rules for access to sensitive data on the information network have been determined, there still remains the age-old problem: who guards the guardians? As an information system of the size we contemplate requires expert programmers to set it up and to maintain it, does it not also create a new and potentially dangerous technological elite? What is to stop these programmers from fixing the information system so that it works to the advantage of their own interests or those of their friends and associates?

Even though there is no foolproof solution to this problem, procedures can be instituted so that programmers independently check random portions of one another's work, without either the original programmers or the checkers knowing when portions are being checked. Beyond this it can only be hoped that most programmers, like most elected officials, will have been socialized to carry out their work in a conscientious and honest manner, not an unreasonable hope in a liberal-democratic polity.

How is all of this to be paid for? A computerized information network does not spring up overnight; it has capitalization costs for computer hardware and developmental costs for programming the software. After it comes into being, it has additional costs for operation and for maintenance, plus further programming costs for updating and improving the software.

If, as seems likely, the network is linked to private homes via television cable, much of the initial capitalization costs will be picked up by community-cable television companies, which are already engaged in setting up local television channels supported by user subscriptions and sometimes commercial advertising. In the United States cable companies already reach over 10 per cent of all households, and they are expected to reach a majority sometime in the 1980s. Although current cable-television broadcasts consist largely of enhancing and then relaying signals of commercial television stations for purposes of entertainment, the Federal Communications Commission has required that all cable networks established since 1972 have a two-way communications capability.[13] Cable television in Britain remains in the trial stage, experimental channels having been set up in only a few cities: Bristol, Sheffield, Wellingborough, Greenwich, Swindon, and Milton Keynes. Whilst these cable channels have experienced difficulty – indeed by mid 1976, they had already closed down in Bristol, Sheffield and Wellingborough – the report of the Annan Committee on the Future of Broadcasting, with its emphasis on local broadcasting authorities for radio and easy public access to a fourth national television channel, may well stimulate renewed interest in local cable television as a possible means for achieving local diversity combined with easy access to TV.[14] Capitalization for an information network in Britain could come in large part from the new channel if it were launched as a commercial-cable television venture. But the Annan Committee does not favour pay television. Indeed if the committee's timetable is followed, the capitalization necessary for setting up a national information network via cable will not be made available until the turn of the century![15]

Once a network is established, basic operating costs could be covered through user fees in much the same way Britain licenses radio and television reception, or American cable companies currently offer their services. If usage of the network proves costly, then steps would have to be taken to assure that poorer citizens were not frozen out. As has sometimes been done with telephone rates in the United States, a low monthly fee could be charged for up to a set number of information units. Beyond this limit, users would have to pay their own information-processing costs. Toll-free public access could be made available at public libraries, however, again to assure that a citizen's financial condition would not become a severe barrier to his participation in politics.

The purpose of this section has been to describe the basic details of a computerized information network. This type of network forms the key element of our theory of viable democracy. It is through such a network that ordinary citizens and – most importantly–their elected representatives should be able to secure the information necessary to make intelligent informed decisions about public policy. By placing relevant information files of both governmental and private bureaucracies on the network, it is hoped that the disadvantage citizens and their elected officials have had in dealing with these technological elites might be overcome. But in using the network to remedy this imbalance of power we have cautioned against the unfettered distribution of personal data, a circumstance which would lead to the sacrifice of personal rights of privacy – liberalism – for the promise of greater political participation – democracy. Instead we have recommended a balanced strategy, which makes all relevant information available to elected representatives, but limits its distribution to the general public. At the same time we have recommended procedures by means of which citizens can monitor, challenge, and have corrected all personal information about themselves that goes on the network.

Of course an information network, no matter how carefully conceived, does not make a viable democracy. Political institutions and laws are required which serve to actuate the potentialities of the network. In addition a certain amount of faith in the rational good will of the citizens and their representatives is required, a faith not incompatible with empirical findings of political science, but not entirely supported by them either. To these additional requirements we now turn.

3

A Theory of Viable Democracy, Part Two: Laws, Institutions and People. Access to politically relevant information is a necessary but not sufficient condition for viable democracy. To produce a viable democracy certain procedural and institutional changes must be added. In this section we discuss four major reforms, which, when combined with the information network, may provide sufficient impetus for a viable democracy. First, in so far as practicable, public-policy questions should be handled by the smallest unit of government capable of resolving them. Secondly, government should take steps to encourage responsible 'whistle-blowing', that is, to encourage responsible individuals to come forth with evidence of abuses of public trust or the common interest by agencies of government or powerful private groups of which they themselves are members. Thirdly, representatives of the general public should be appointed to the policy-making boards of groups which have their computerized files on the network, in order to encourage the injection of public interest as opposed to special group interest into their decisions. And fourthly, new methods of accounting should be instituted, methods which take account of the costs of environmental pollution, resource depletion, and the maintenance of the publicly financed infrastructure that provides goods, services and trained individuals to business and industry.

The first reform comports with major findings of political

science as well as some long-established traditions in democratic theory. In addition it also has some implications for dealing with problems of limited environmental resources of the sort we discussed in chapter 6.

Normally it is easier for individual citizens or groups to influence the policy-making decisions of smaller local units of government than those of larger distant ones. To begin with, an individual citizen's vote has a significantly greater probability of deciding the outcome of a local election than a national one; and a bloc of votes cast by his group or party will have an even greater probability of being decisive. Between elections most local representatives and bureaucrats will be easier to reach than will national ones. And the costs of conducting an educational or propaganda campaign among the relevant electorate will be considerably less than would be the case for a larger unit of government.

Citizens perceive they usually have a better chance of influencing the decisions of local government than they do those of other more distant governments. Studies have shown that on average citizens feel more efficacious regarding their dealings with local political problems than they do with national ones. Citizens also tend to distrust local officials less than others. And in general citizens find the business of local government more comprehensible than that of regional, state and national governments.[16]

Several traditions of democratic theory have long extolled the virtues of smaller units of government or, indeed, of eliminating formal governmental institutions altogether. Rousseau argued that any governmental unit so large that it required representative rather than direct participation bred citizen apathy, invited corruption and threatened destruction of liberty.[17] The Utopian socialists tended to favour small autonomous polities led by scientific and technological elites, not elected representatives. In the Marxist communist state the government withered away, and participation in collective decision-making became direct. Although Madison and the American Federalists favoured representative government, they emphasized the importance of state and local government as a check against usurpation of power by national government. In their view state and local governments

served as bulwarks of liberty. Anarchists like Kropotkin emphasized the essential democracy of small autonomous communes,
in which all citizens worked to solve problems cooperatively. And
even today those who argue in favour of greater devolution or
community control contend that these reforms will make the
polity more democratic.

Finally, the idea of concentrating greater decision-making
power in smaller units of government accords with the recent
thinking of critics of bigness like Robert Dahl, John Galbraith,
Amory Lovins, Morton Mintz, and E. F. Schumacher.[18] Although their emphases differ, all of these critics point out that
too often governmental and industrial units have become so
large that economies of scale have ceased to operate, and the
flexibility required for dealing with peculiar local problems has
also been lost.

An industrial conglomerate usually is no more efficient than
its separate companies, and these companies in turn have no
better efficiency rates than do their separate plants. Indeed, because of their lower capitalization costs, smaller firms often show
greater facility for adopting small-scale technological innovations
and for adapting processes to accommodate local demands than
do larger ones. Services or products offered on a smaller scale
through numerous firms or units may prove of better quality
than those offered on a large scale by fewer units, even when the
large-scale offerings appear less costly. Small-scale electrical generating plants integrated in a grid, for instance, are less likely to
trigger a massive breakdown of the grid than are a few large
ones. And when breakdowns do occur, they are easier to fix.
Moreover, if the plant which generates power for a community
is located in that community, instead of some distance away,
citizens will become more aware of the immediate trade-offs involved between, say, increased generating capacity and increased
environmental pollution. With plants serving smaller communities the citizens might also be better able to judge which services
should be given high priorities and what rate structures should
be adopted for customer payment.[19]

The same sorts of considerations apply to services provided
by government. It is questionable whether there are any signifi-

cant economies of scale to be derived from providing most services under the direction of one central unit, once cities have grown much beyond 250,000 in population. The city of New York certainly does not provide more efficient services for its nearly 8 million inhabitants than does the city of Dayton, Ohio, for its quarter million people. It has been argued with some cogency that New York City would provide far better government if it functioned as a state with a number of autonomous local governments, instead of as the essentially centralized unit it is today.[20] Similar criticism has been applied lately to the centralized government of the United Kingdom; as a result considerable reform in the structures and powers of local and regional government has already taken place and more is expected.

This does not mean that large units in government or industry are inherently bad. But it does suggest that the decision-making scope of these units should be limited to those problems which cannot be handled well by smaller units. These would include such problems as control of environmental pollution, explorations of the ocean floor and of outer space, and the underwriting of defence projects requiring heavy capital investment.

The proposed information network should provide considerable help to local governmental units in deciding upon and implementing policy. If local governments have at hand the recorded experience of other governmental units in dealing with analogous political problems, this should not only enhance their capability to deal with these problems, but it should also improve the effectiveness of the policies that are implemented.

Even if information is accessible to the general public, there is still no guarantee that it will be employed to serve that public. The information may never be accessed; if it is accessed, it may be ignored or perhaps exploited for private advantage. Nor can elected officials be expected to become aware of all the pertinent information accessible which bears upon current questions of public policy. MPs and Congressmen readily admit that the business of modern government is so broad and so complex that at any given moment it is nearly impossible for one representative to absorb major portions of the relevant information on more than a few matters of public policy. Even though an astute staff can greatly increase a legislator's capacity to absorb such information, it is inevitable that important bits will be missed.[21] Some information will be ignored, because it is too complex for the legislator or his staff to comprehend; other information will be ignored, because its relevance to the legislator's public policy concerns is not immediately apparent; and some will be missed altogether, because the sheer volume of information forces legislators to review only a portion of it.

Legislators must rely upon interested citizens, therefore, to call their attention to some important problems. This is already the case to a certain extent. Legislators rely upon the testimony of experts directly via committee hearings and lobbying activities and also indirectly via advisory boards to executive agencies. In addition the proposed information network will make it easier for other interested citizens to offer their testimonies. Yet all this is still insufficient. Incentives are needed to encourage experts within the bureaucracies, both public and private, to place regard for the common interest over and above their usual loyalties to peer groups. These experts must be induced to come forward with information about activities in their agencies or organizations which they deem contrary to the common interest.[22] In other words a viable democracy must encourage responsible 'whistle-blowing'.

If a manufacturing firm surreptitiously pollutes a stream, fails to recall a potentially dangerous product, or suppresses an apparently beneficial invention, we would like to know. If a welfare agency deliberately misapplies a law, if a defence agency makes unauthorized expenditures, or if a military unit secretly disobeys orders, we would like to know. But it is usually only those within the offending organizations who have the technical expertise and the information to bring the matter to public attention.

And there are strong pressures against revealing this very information. First the social interaction of group enterprise fosters a certain level of loyalty to the group. It is considered unethical – even childish – to run to higher authority bearing tales of the group's every misdeed, however trivial. And with good reason, for every organization inevitably makes some errors in its work.

The mark of a responsible individual is the ability to distinguish trivial or unintentional errors from serious or deliberate misdeeds. And if a responsible individual chooses to report upon his organization's misdeeds to higher authority, he must have the maturity and self-confidence to withstand the criticisms of those who will impugn his concern for the public interest and excoriate him for betraying his peers.[23]

In addition to normal social pressures, however, the modern polity provides some definite disincentives for those who contemplate 'blowing the whistle' on their organizations. Although the welfare state provides some basic benefits for all citizens, those who work for bureaucratic organizations usually become eligible to receive attractive supplementary benefits. These include private pension plans, health and medical benefits, and group insurances of various sorts. A person who tells on his organization risks losing all these benefits through being sacked in retaliation for his disloyalty. Thus the economic benefits conferred by group status serve to reinforce primal group loyalties.

A viable democracy, therefore, must act to protect the economic well-being of whistle-blowers. By law government should guarantee the pension rights, group insurances, and other fringe benefits of those who come forward with responsible criticism of their organizations. Government should also outlaw economic retaliation, particularly in the form of job discrimination, by affected organizations or agencies against those who report on them. (Discrimination may be so subtle that in the end government itself may have to guarantee employment for these individuals.)

Yet care must also be taken not to encourage frivolous or irresponsible tattling. Guidelines for responsible whistle-blowing should be developed appropriate to the circumstances of each polity. Data on the information network should make it easier to verify or disprove any charges of misconduct that are made.

It would be far more desirable if organizations and agencies could be induced to act more responsibly in the common interest from the start. Let us consider how this sort of behaviour might be encouraged.

Regarding government itself, no radical changes are needed other than improving citizens' ability to monitor the activities of executive agencies by instituting the information network described above. Liberal government is supposed to serve the interests of its citizenry. Its purpose is to secure individual rights and liberties (social contract) or to secure the greatest happiness for the greatest number (utilitarianism). Thus, if citizens elect responsible officials, and means are provided for them to monitor the behaviour of these officials, there will be ample incentive for such officials to act in the common interest.

To induce private corporations or even nationalized enterprises to act in the common interest will require additional reforms. The most important of these is placement of one or more public representatives onto the policy-making boards of these corporations. The purpose of the public representatives will be to inject into policy deliberations considerations other than those which benefit the corporation, its workers, and its clientele. In order to accomplish their purpose these representatives will need to resist the group pressures towards cooptation as an ordinary member of the board. To this end the terms of service of public representatives should be of limited duration with limited possibilities of renewal, and their salaries should be paid out of public funds. (Representatives who serve on boards of nationalized enterprises should be paid out of funds separate from those of regular members of the board.) Rules should also be adopted forbidding those who have served as public representatives to serve in turn as regular members of the same boards.

As public representatives would have access to all relevant corporation records to which regular board members have access, they would be at least as well prepared as others to argue their case. The relationship of policy-making boards to management in a corporation is similar to that between legislators and bureaucrats in government; the latter often have the knowledge and expertise to manipulate the decisions of the former.[24] But with the increased power provided by the information network, a public representative will probably have a better chance of raising considerations of the common interest than at present. Furthermore, the presence of public representatives on corporate boards may encourage responsible whistle-blowing by members of management, for the representatives would provide within the corporation a non-hostile authority predisposed to investigate any allegations of misconduct.

Public representatives should also be appointed to the boards of large unions and eventually, if government thinks it appropriate, to the boards of all organizations and agencies whose computerized records become part of the information network. The overall aim in making these appointments is to inject considerations of the common interest as opposed to selfish interest into the deliberations of these bodies.

The idea of injecting such considerations into the policy making of non-governmental organizations is not really radical. Governments have often tried to induce business and labour organizations to act more responsibly, for example, by calling for voluntary restraints on prices and wages. The Labour Government under Mr Wilson and Mr Callaghan has made these considerations explicit by elevating voluntary wage restraints by unions to the level of a 'Social Contract', wherein government in turn endeavours to keep prices within certain bounds of inflation. Even more explicit are rules regarding product safety and quality, safety of the workplace, minimum standards for wages and hours, and rules for negotiation of contracts between labour and management. The appointment of public representatives to the boards of these organizations simply attempts to raise considerations of the common interest from the inside instead of imposing them from the outside.

The closest working models of the sort of responsible self-governance of organizations that we have in mind are the Yugoslavian workers' councils, which form the fundamental managerial units for corporate enterprise in that country. These councils set the wages and conditions for the plant. They also work out the budgets and overall five-year plans. They select a managing board for day to day supervision of operations and they also select the plant director. The selection of the director is not made with only selfish considerations of the enterprise in mind. An equal number of representatives from the municipality in which the plant operates serve on the committee that chooses a director; certain of the director's subsequent decisions can be appealed to the government of the municipality; and the same committee that hired the director can ultimately sack him. Thus considerations of the plant's effect on the community form a routine part of the policy-making process.[25]

Although the Yugoslavian enterprises, whose employees usually number under 1,000, are too small to be directly comparable to the huge multinational corporations, they are often comparable to the separate plants of these corporations. This suggests that in order to encourage the operation of non-governmental organizations in the common interest, we should extend our first reform to these organizations: policy questions of large organizations, such as corporations, should, as much as possible, be handled by the smallest organizational unit capable of deciding them. If local plants are given a greater degree of autonomy, they are likely to become more exposed to community pressures and then more responsive to the interests of the communities in which they operate.[26] One important additional service that public representatives on the boards of these organizations may render will be to work toward decentralization of decision-making structures of these organizations.

The fourth major reform, the institution of new methods of accounting, which include environmental costs as well as the costs of private appropriation of publicly financed goods and services, is technically the easiest to accomplish. As government already sets standards of accounting in order to assess taxes, it will break no precedents for it simply to set new ones. Although the content of the standards will vary from polity to polity, the effect of the accounting system will be to sully the notion that the profits of private enterprise arise solely from its own efforts, not also from a fortunate combination of circumstances, namely of easy access to the bounties of nature and the services of government.[27]

If firms have to account for the depletion of natural resources, this should provide an incentive to conserve these resources and to exploit them in ways that make the most use of them, not necessarily in ways that are the most economically efficient under the current methods of accounting. If business and labour have to account for the value of the services of government, not only will they be conscious of how tax monies are spent, but they should also be more concerned about the appropriateness and the effectiveness of these expenditures. It is to be hoped, then, that the institution of the new accounting system will have the side benefit of encouraging citizens to take increased interest in the activities of government.

4

Alternatives to Viable Democracy. The theory of viable democracy stated above describes a form of government which satisfies the major criteria for a liberal democracy. The proposed information network provides substantial equal access to political information for all citizens. Where considerations of individual privacy or national security require limitations of general public access, the citizens' elected representatives are nonetheless allowed access to the restricted information. Thanks to the information network, citizens and their representatives have the means to acquire the knowledge necessary for meaningful participation in all aspects of politics.

Moreover, through the network's facility to communicate information to designated target populations, the power of ordinary citizens and their representatives to place items on the public agenda is greatly enhanced. By means of the network citizens can communicate their opinions on matters of public policy to their elected representatives, relevant government administrators, relevant interest groups, and members of the general public interested in the area of policy. Nor need the communications run only one way. Elected representatives and other government officials can call matters to the attention of relevant constituent groups as well.

In addition to the network the theory posits a number of political reforms – decentralization, whistle-blowing, public representatives for the common interest, and new methods of accounting – all designed to provide citizens and their representatives with the capability to exert some control over the major political and social institutions of the polity.

Finally, even though the theory does posit a degree of rationality among the citizenry, which is not entirely supported by the findings of political science, it nonetheless makes no unrealistic demands in terms of the time and the interest required of ordinary citizens in order for a viable democracy to function.

No system of government is without flaws, and viable democracy of course is no exception. We have already discussed some potential problems, such as the abuse of privileged information by elected representatives or clever programmers, and the practical difficulties of developing a comprehensive information network that is both simple and cheap to use. We can also anticipate several other problems: frivolous instances of whistle-blowing that take up time and tax money; absurd and petty squabbles over policy among decentralized governmental authorities; co-optation or corruption of public representatives on corporate boards; and inaccurate or absurd formulae for estimating the costs of depletion of natural resources or provision of government services. Nevertheless we believe that in comparison to other more conventional statements of liberal democracy, viable democracy stands up well. In this section we examine five such statements commonly touted as reforms designed to liberalize and democratize modern government. These are: increased participation, increased legislative power, increased regulatory power, anarchism and socialism. After examining each alternative, we shall explain our reasons for preferring viable democracy.

In their common form arguments for increased participation stress the importance of maintaining high levels of citizen interest and activity. They usually recommend greater participation in interest groups, more frequent communication with representatives by conventional means (letters, telegrams and petitions), and greater attention to public affairs as reported by the mass media. Increased coverage of political events is urged upon the mass media, and more frequent referenda and more frequent elections are sometimes also recommended.[28]

Unfortunately the average citizen simply is not prepared to live up to the high levels of participation expected by those who advocate these reforms. As we have seen, most citizens ordinarily have neither the time nor the inclination to spend more than minimal effort on all but the few political issues which affect them most directly. But even if they were as inclined towards political activity as our own Good Citizen Brown, they would find it as impossible as he did to keep up with most political developments, given the current nexus of political institutions. The hope of achieving liberal democracy simply by urging greater citizen participation in politics is an unrealistic one. At the very least, the blandishments of increased political participation must be accompanied by proposals for meaningful legal and institutional reforms, perhaps along the lines of those we have already proposed.

Arguments for increased legislative power are usually based upon the premise that the legislature, usually the only body of representatives elected by the people, ought to maintain a fundamental policy-making role. To achieve this end greater salaries are urged for legislators in order to attract representatives who are better qualified to lead. Beyond this, increased staffs are urged, both for individual legislators and their committees, in order to provide expertise needed to help plan programmes and control the executive. Finally specialization in one or two areas of policy is urged upon each legislator.[29]

While nothing seems objectionable about these reforms per se, they will probably prove inadequate without accompanying institutional reforms like those proposed in our theory of viable democracy. We can pay high salaries to attract qualified men and women to office; we can increase staffs to provide better information to these men and women; we can urge legislators to specialize; but we still must confront the fact that bureaucrats almost always have better information than legislators about a subject. Unless we are willing to urge staff expansions on a truly massive scale, it is absurd to expect legislators to gain sufficient expertise to match the information possessed by interest groups or the executive concerning most questions of public policy. Yet to urge such expansions would be equally absurd, for it would turn the legislature into a massive costly institution, which would tend to duplicate the work of the executive. It seems more sensible to recommend development of an information network of the type we have already proposed and to supplement this network with legislation that encourages and protects whistle-blowers.

Where expansion of legislative power emphasizes the importance of the elected representative, expansion of regulatory power emphasizes the importance of the qualified administrator. Elected officials tend to be concerned about reelection. As a result they often choose the popular alternative rather than the correct one, when it comes to making a tough policy decision. Yet many government activities, such as running the postal service or publicly owned utilities; regulating the stock market, money markets, or banks; arbitrating labour disputes; or developing weapons systems call for tough decisions requiring technical expertise, not posturing for votes. The solution proposed here is to 'hive off' various areas of administrative decision-making from direct interference by the legislature. Expert administrators should be given general directions, and then left to their own devices to achieve – sometimes even to determine – the desired goals.[30]

Here we return once again to a fundamental question of democratic theory. Do the experts really know what is better for the citizens than do the citizens themselves or their representatives? We doubt it, but we must admit that this doubt is based largely on faith, not conclusive evidence. For every failure of bureaucratic expertise, such as that of the Department of Economic Affairs in Britain, we can find a comparable legislative failure, such as Congressional interference with management of the Post Office Department before it became a public corporation. Finally, we share the liberal democrat's belief that, given the appropriate information, citizens or their elected representatives can decide as wisely as anyone else upon matters of public policy. For this reason we still prefer the reforms proposed in our theory of viable democracy to those which confer more power upon the administrative experts.

Although the term 'anarchism' is out of fashion these days, the idea of small self-sufficient communes remains popular in both fact and fiction.[31] Aided by the advances of modern technology, self-governing, virtually self-sufficient communes flourish today even more easily than in the past. And as anarchists have long pointed out, they suffer none of the dangers of dominancy by a remote government inherent in the institutional structures of modern mass polities. The successful anarchist commune is probably the closest thing to pure direct democracy that modern man has achieved.

But is this form of democracy generalizable to the mass public? It seems highly doubtful that more than a select minority of modern men would choose to dissociate themselves from their familiar habits of governance in order to reorganize into communes. The vast majority seem comfortable with present institutional forms. That is why we believe that the decentralization of power among established governmental units, as advocated in our theory, represents a more viable reform than does the anarchist's commune.

From our present perspective the objection to socialism as a modern democratic reform is its lack of relevance for solving problems like citizen control of large and powerful bureaucracies or preservation of the environment. Socialism, we recall, first emerged as a critique of eighteenth- and nineteenth-century liberal-democratic institutions.[32] The central point of this critique was that liberal democracy's guarantees of political freedom were essentially empty without a fundamental redistribution of property. At bottom political freedom was built upon a materialistic foundation. The socialists grasped that the emerging industries could provide the wherewithal needed for every citizen to realize his potential – to develop himself to the fullest – in short, to exercise his political freedom. But under the capitalist mode of economic organization, the average citizen, the proletarian, never got to enjoy the fruits of his labour, for they were appropriated by the capitalist.

In the modern industrial state, however, material prosperity – a decent standard of living – has become general enough for this critique to have lost much of its bite. To a certain extent the capitalists have reformed: they provide better pay, safer working conditions, health and welfare benefits. And to a certain extent socialists have adopted capitalist economic concerns: state-owned enterprises fret over production rates, squabble with their workers over wages, and pollute the air and the water just as if they were privately owned. In fact, with regard to concern for quality of life it is difficult to distinguish an avowedly capitalist polity like the United States from an avowedly socialist one like Britain. As E. F. Schumacher has pointed out:

> Ownership, whether public or private, is merely an element of a framework. It does not by itself settle the kind of objectives to be pursued within the framework ... There is therefore really no strong case for public ownership if the objectives to be pursued by nationalised industries are to be just as narrow, just as limited, as those of capitalist production: profitability and nothing else. Herein lies the real danger to nationalisation in Britain at the present time, not in any imagined inefficiency ... What is at stake is not economics but culture, not the standard of living but the quality of life. Economics and standard of living can just as well be looked after by a capitalist system, moderated by a bit of planning and redistributive taxation. But culture and, generally, the quality of life, can now only be debased by such a system.[33]

The reforms advocated in our theory of viable democracy are designed to address these problems while ordinary statements which advocate socialism are not. Nationalization is an entirely separate issue from the reforms we propose. Viable democracy could function regardless of whether all the polity's industry were publicly owned or private. It could not function without an information network, decentralized governmental decision-making, encouragement of whistle-blowing, public-interest representatives to serve on the boards of large enterprises (both public and private), and methods of accounting that take into consideration quality of life items like environmental pollution, resource depletion and the provision of publicly supported goods and services.

Although we prefer our theory of viable democracy to the above-discussed reforms, we make no claim that the reforms described by the theory are the only ones that will serve to implement the values of liberal democracy in the modern industrial state. We do contend that reforms which simply urge more of some desirable action or policy – more participation, more legislative staff, more bureaucratic expertise, more communes, more nationalization – will fail if they do not also include modifications of the structures and operations of traditional political institutions.

Liberal democracy in the last decades of the twentieth century cannot be realized merely by streamlining the political institutions of the eighteenth and nineteenth centuries. As Marcuse tells us at the head of this chapter, 'new modes of realization are needed, corresponding to the new capabilities of society.'[34] That viable democracy implements some of these new capabilities is another reason why we prefer it to more traditional reforms like those discussed above. Such traditional reforms can surely be modified so as to account for new social capabilities. But for the nonce the reforms proposed by our theory seem more likely to produce a viable liberal democracy.

5

Prospects for Success. The theory of viable democracy is not set forth merely as an intellectual flight of fancy. Granted, the theory makes some optimistic assumptions about the rationality of political behaviour; granted, the reforms advocated in the theory contain potential hazards for liberal democracy as well as potential benefits. Nonetheless, we do not believe it is fatally flawed. If the theory were implemented, we think it would work. The real problem will be to secure its implementation.

To begin with there is no evidence of substantial numbers of citizens clamouring for reform. Despite their growing distrust of government in general and politicians in particular, most citizens still give strong support to the governing institutions of their polities. Most Americans congratulate themselves on how well their democratic political system works, notwithstanding the dismissal of President Nixon and Vice President Agnew and the ascension of Gerald Ford to the Presidency without election. Whether used effectively or not, the powers of the British Parliament are still so revered that sufficient support cannot be mustered for instituting even modest devolutionary reforms ceding some independent powers to regional parliaments in Scotland and Wales.

But let us suppose that our arguments were so convincing that after a time a majority of citizens came to believe that major reforms of the sort we have suggested were needed in order to implement viable democratic governance. And let us further suppose that capitalization of a national cable-television network proceeded apace so that the instrumentality for instituting the central reform was already at hand. There still might be insufficient motivation for any substantial number of ordinary citizens to seek these reforms, for past experience indicates that the chances of achieving major reforms, as opposed to incremental ones, are really rather minute. A realistic estimate of the amount of time required to achieve such reforms by means of a series of incremental changes – perhaps a decade or more – would discourage all but the most dedicated of political activists.[35]

We struggle forward towards viable democracy as if on a treadmill. To move from elitist dominated politics towards viable democratic governance we need major political reforms. We cannot institute major reforms without widespread citizen support. We cannot gain widespread citizen support so long as our politics is dominated by elites who favour the *status quo* or, at most, incremental change. At the least, progress towards implementing viable liberal democracy will proceed very slowly.

We are frankly pessimistic about the future of liberal democracy. Far from adopting our viable democratic reforms, it seems likely that industrial nations of the West will continue to conduct politics in the customary manner. Traditional liberal-democratic institutions like legislatures will continue to be dominated by newer governing elites: the public bureaucracy, the military planners, and the corporate managers. The public policies pursued will continue to reflect outmoded assumptions of the costlessness of depleting our natural resources and polluting our natural environment. Changes in policy will be implemented in an orderly incremental fashion. Economic growth and the concomitant rise in the material standards of living of most citizens will remain the overriding goals of public policy.

Only when the resources that have sustained this growth have nearly run out will any radical adjustments in policy occur. For the citizens' own good these adjustments will be imposed upon them by experts from the governing elite, based upon information to which only the experts are privy. The policies imposed may or may not be successful in terms of maintaining standards of living, but the policy process will be neither liberal nor democratic. And to the extent that citizen participation in the political decision-making contributes to their self-development and sense of responsibility to the community, the quality of life will have declined.

There are other dangers as well. It is trite but true that the concentration of political power in the hands of a few tends to corrupt those few. If it turns out that the average standards of living must decline, why should the leadership choose to suffer along with *hoi polloi*? Having expertise is not the same as having concern for the common interest.

These pessimistic conclusions derive from the head, however, not from the heart. Liberal democracy has always required a leap of faith, a belief in men as rational beings, capable not only of deciding what is best for themselves as individuals but also what is best for themselves as a community. We have presented one theory of how political institutions and processes can be arranged – viable democracy – so that citizens can cope with today's governmental responsibilities in a liberal-democratic fashion. The theory makes that leap of faith: it presumes the basic rationality of the citizenry. But it does not make the unrealistic demand that every citizen conform to the Athenian ideal. It is, we believe, a reasonable – indeed, viable – proposition. If it serves to inspire new efforts to bring about liberal-democratic reform, we shall be gratified.

Notes

Introduction (pp. 7–16)

1. cf. Dorothy Pickles, *Democracy*, Methuen, 1971; Ernest Barker, *Reflections on Government*, Oxford University Press, 1942; Harold Laski, *A Grammar of Politics*, Allen & Unwin, 1930.
2. cf. Bernard Berelson *et al.*, *Voting*, Chicago University Press, Chicago, 1954; Gabriel Almond and Sidney Verba, *The Civic Culture*, Little, Brown & Co., Boston, 1965; Lester Milbrath, *Political Participation*, Rand McNally, Chicago, 1965.
3. cf. John Playford and Charles McCoy, eds., *Apolitical Politics*, Thomas Crowell, New York, 1965; William Connolly, ed., *The Bias of Pluralism*, Aldine-Atherton, Chicago, 1969; Henry Kariel, ed., *Frontiers of Democratic Theory*, Random House, New York, 1970; John Plamenatz, *Democracy and Illusion*, Longman, 1973. Exceptions are: Dennis F. Thompson, *The Democratic Citizen*, Cambridge University Press, 1970; Carole Bateman, *Participation and Democratic Theory*, Cambridge University Press, 1970; C. B. Macpherson, *The Life and Times of Liberal Democracy*, Oxford University Press, 1977.

Chapter 1: Politics, Democracy, Political Science (pp. 17–25)

1. Hans J. Morganthau, *Politics Among Nations*, fourth edition, A. A. Knopf, New York, 1967; Harold D. Lasswell and Abraham Kaplan, *Power and Society: A Framework for Political Inquiry*, Yale University Press, New Haven, 1963; C. Wright Mills, *The Power Elite*, Oxford University Press, New York, 1956.
2. Arthur Bentley, *The Process of Government*, University of Chicago Press, 1908; Charles Merriam, *Political Power*, McGraw-Hill, New York, 1932; David Truman, *The Governmental Process*, A. A. Knopf, New York, 1951.
3. David Easton, *The Political System*, A. A. Knopf, New York, 1971; Harold Lasswell, *Politics: Who Gets What, When, How*, World Publishers, New York, 1958.

4. Karl Deutsch, *Nerves of Government*, Free Press, New York, 1963; Talcott Parsons, 'An Outline of the Social System', in Parsons *et al.*, *The Uses of Society*, Free Press, New York, 1961.
5. Almond and Verba, pp. 246–51; Norman Nie and Sidney Verba, *Participation in America*, Harper & Row, New York, 1972, chapter 2; David Butler and Donald Stokes, *Political Change in Britain*, Penguin Books, Harmondsworth, 1971, chapters 2, 6, 7.
6. Theodore Roosevelt, *The Rough Riders*, 1899; reproduction of 1899 edition, Williamstown, New Corner House, 1971; Jacobus Ten Broek, *Prejudice, War and the Constitution*, University of California Press, Berkeley, 1952.
7. The two books in question are *August 1914*, Bodley Head, 1972; and *The Gulag Archipelago*, Penguin Books, Harmondsworth, 1974.
8. cf. Adam Przeworski and Henry Teune, *The Logic of Comparative Social Inquiry*, John Wiley & Sons, New York, 1970.

Chapter 2: Liberal Democracy (pp. 26–43)

1. cf. C. B. Macpherson, *The Real World of Democracy*, Oxford University Press, 1966, chapters 1–3.
2. The quotation is from the 'Declaration of Independence'.
3. See his letter to William S. Smith, 13 November 1787 in Carl Cohen, ed., *Communism, Fascism and Democracy*, Random House, New York, 1962. For a thesis that Jefferson derived his political philosophy from the Scottish moralists, not Locke, see Garry Wills, *Inventing America: Jefferson's Declaration of Independence*, Doubleday, Garden City, N. Y., 1978, part 3. For the standard Lockean thesis, see Carl L. Becker, *The Declaration of Independence*, A. A. Knopf, New York, 1966, chapter 2.
4. *Leviathan*, Part I, chapter 13.
5. *The Social Contract*, chapter 1.
6. *ibid.*, chapter 3.
7. *ibid.*, chapter 6.
8. *ibid.*, chapter 7.
9. The electoral reforms bringing about virtually universal manhood suffrage for whites were accomplished in the United States in the 1820s. See A. T. Mason, ed., *Free Government in the Making*, Oxford University Press, 1965, Part X, 382 ff.
10. *On Liberty*, chapter 1.
11. *Utilitarianism*, chapter 2.
12. *Considerations of Representative Government*, chapter 1.

13. The principle of balanced government is at least as old as Aristotle's *Politics* (384–22 B.C.), but its modern statement was developed by Baron Charles de Secondat Montesquieu in his *Esprit des Lois* (*Spirit of the Laws*) first published in 1748.

Chapter 3 Critiques of Liberal Democracy (pp. 44–69)

1. Burke, *Reflections*, 1970, in Louis I. Brevold and Ralph G. Ross, eds., *The Philosophy of Edmund Burke*, University of Michigan Press, Ann Arbor, 1960, p. 43.
2. Burke, *Thoughts on the Cause of the Present Discontents* (1770), in Brevold and Ross, p. 138. The observation originated with Aristotle's *Politics*. Aristotle lived 384–22 B.C.
3. 'Speech to the Electors of Bristol', 4 November 1974.
4. 'Speech on Mr Fox's East India Bill', 1 December 1783, in Brevold and Ross, p. 156.
5. Kant's principal works on these themes were *Critique of Pure Reason*, 1781, *Critique of Practical Reason*, 1787, and *Metaphysics of Morality*, 1784.
6. cf. *Metaphysics of Morality*, section 2.
7. Smith's great treatise, *The Wealth of Nations*, was first published in 1776.
8. Spencer introduced the notion of survival of the fittest in his *Social Statics* first published in 1855 some four years before the appearance of Darwin's *On the Origin of Species*.
9. Saint-Simon developed his ideas on religion in *The New Christianity*, 1825.
10. Marx and Engels, *The German Ideology*, Part 1, written in 1845–6, this work was not published until the 1940s. See Carl Cohen, op. cit., p. 76.
11. For an introduction to Marxian economic theory, see J. B. Sanderson, *An Interpretation of the Political Ideas of Marx and Engels*, Longmans, Green, 1969, chapter 3.
12. Marx and Engels, *The Communist Manifesto*, 1848.
13. Lenin of course adapted the ideas of Marx and Engels to suit the current needs of the Russian revolutionaries. Of particular importance was his introduction of the communist party as the vanguard of the proletariat. For a survey of Marxian literature, see *The Essential Left*, Unwin Books, 1971.
14. The principles underlying these three branches of government were developed by Montesquieu, op. cit.
15. James Madison, Alexander Hamilton and John Jay, *The Federal-*

ist Papers, nos. 14, 39, 52; Jill, *Representative Government*, chapter 3.

16. Rousseau, *The Social Contract*, chapter 15.

17. Cole's major statements of guild socialism appeared in *Self Government in Industry*, 1917, *Social Theory*, 1920 and *Guild Socialism restated*, 1921.

18. Quoted in Margaret Spahr, *Readings in Recent Political Philosophy*, Macmillan, New York, 1935.

19. Bakunin's work is scattered. For a selection in English see G. R. Maxinoff, ed., *The Political Philosophy of Bakunin: Scientific Anarchism*, The Free Press, Glencoe, Ill., 1953. Kropotkin's major works included *The Conquest of Bread*, 1892, *Mutual Aid*, 1896, and *Fields, Factories and Workshops*, 1899.

20. Mosca's contemporary Vilfredo Pareto (1848–1923) developed a sociological theory which was in many ways similar to Mosca's élitism. On the bad blood between them see James H. Meisel, *The Myth of the Ruling Class*, Ann Arbor, University of Michigan Press, 1962, chapter 8.

21. *Political Parties*, Part VI, chapter 1.

22. cf. John Stuart Mill, *Principles of Political Economy* (1848), Book V, chapter 11.

23. Bernstein's major work, *Evolutionary Socialism*, was first published in Germany in 1899.

24. Translated from *Fédéralisme, Socialisme et Antithéologisme* in Alexander Gray, *The Socialism Tradition: Moses to Lenin*, Longmans, Green, 1946, p. 359.

Chapter 4: Liberal Democracy in the Twentieth Century (pp. 70–94)

1. H. L. Mencken, *Notes on Democracy*, A. A. Knopf, New York, 1926, p. 59.

2. ibid., p. 169.

3. cf. George Sabine, *A History of Political Theory*, Holt, Rinehart & Winston, New York, 1960, pp. 870–74; Carl Cohen, ed., *Communism, Fascism and Democracy: The Theoretical Foundations*, Random House, New York, 1972, sections 47, 54 and 56.

4. Carl Cohen, ed., *Communism, Fascism and Democracy: The Theoretical Foundations*, first edition, Random House, New York, 1962, p. 418, quoted from a speech by Adolf Hitler, Munich, 18 July 1922 and published in *Völkischer Beobachter*, 16 August 1922.

Notes

5. William L. Shirer, *The Rise and Fall of the Third Reich*, Crest Books, New York, 1962, p. 46; quoted from Adolf Hitler, *Mein Kampf*, American edition, Boston, 1943, p. 100.

6. cf. Gabriel Almond and Sidney Verba, *The Civic Culture: Political Attitudes and Democracy in Five Nations*, Princeton University Press, Princeton, 1963, p. 89; David Butler and Donald Stokes, *Political Change in Britain: Forces Shaping Electoral Choice*, St Martin's Press, New York, 1969, pp. 482 and 496; Angus Campbell, Philip E. Converse, Warren E. Miller, and Donald E. Stokes, *The American Voter*, John Wiley & Sons, New York, 1960, p. 103; Arthur Miller and Warren E. Miller, *Election Time-Series Analysis*, (mimeo) Center for Political Studies, Ann Arbor, 1972; William H. Flanigan, *Political Behavior of the American Electorate*, Allyn & Bacon, Boston, 1972, p. 46.

7. cf. Philip E. Converse, Warren E. Miller, Jerrold G. Rusk, and Arthur C. Wolfe, 'Continuity and Change in American Politics: Parties and Issues in the 1968 Election', *American Political Science Review*, LXIII, December 1969, 1101–5.

8. cf. Campbell *et al.*, chapter 15; Seymour Martin Lipset, *Political Man; The Social Bases of Politics*, Anchor Books, Garden City, New York, 1963, pp. 13–15 and 226–9. But see also Dennis Kavenagh, 'Political Behavior and Political Participation', in Garaint Perry, ed., *Political Participation*, Manchester University Press, Manchester, 1972, pp. 102–23.

9. Commission on the Constitution, *Devolution and Other Aspects of Government: An Attitude Survey*, Her Majesty's Stationery Office 1973, pp. 8–9, 156. Only 48 per cent of those Scots interviewed knew of the Scottish Office. The Welsh did slightly better; 56 per cent knew of the Welsh Office, p. 81.

10. Butler and Stokes, pp. 425–7.

11. Ian Budge, J. A. Brand, Michael Margolis, and A. L. M. Smith, *Political Stratification and Democracy*, Macmillan, 1972, pp. 106–7.

12 Mark Abrams, 'Social Trends in Electoral Behavior', in Richard Rose, ed., *Studies in British Politics*, Macmillan, 1966, p. 135.

13. cf. Robert S. Erikson and Norman R. Luttbeg, *American Public Opinion: Its Origins, Content and Impact*, John Wiley & Sons, New York, 1973, p. 25; Stanley R. Freedman, 'The Salience of Party and Candidate in Congressional Elections', in Norman R. Luttbeg, ed., *Public Opinion and Public Policy; Models of Political Linkage*, Dorsey Press, Homewood, Ill., 1974, pp. 126–31;

Dennis J. Palumbo, *American Politics*, Appleton-Century-Crofts, New York, 1973, pp. 357–8.

14. Butler and Stokes, 'Questionnaires', pp. 463–506.

15. Dr George H. Gallup, *The Gallup Poll, Public Opinions 1935–1971*, volume 3, 1959–71, Random House, New York, 1972, p. 1944.

16. cf. *Gallup Poll Index*, January 1974.

17. Gallup, p. 1909; Flanigan, p. 90.

18. Richard Rose, *People in Politics: Observations Across the Atlantic*, Basic Books, New York, 1970, p. 126.

19. *Commission of the Constitution*, pp. 10–12.

20. Campbell *et al.*, p. 174.

21. Gallup, p. 1969.

22. cf. Erikson and Luttbeg, pp. 117–18.

23. Milton J. Rosenberg, Sidney Verba, and Philip E. Converse, *Vietnam and the Silent Majority: The Dove's Guide*, HarRow Books, 1970, pp. 24–5.

24. cf. Hadley Cantril, *The Pattern of Human Concerns*, Rutgers University Press, New Brunswick, New Jersey, 1965, pp. 23, 167–71; Albert H. Cantril and Charles W. Roll, *Hopes and Fears of the American People*, Universe Books, New York, 1971, p. 19; John C. Wahlke, *Public Policy and Representative Government: the Role of the Represented*, Laboratory of Political Research, Iowa City, Iowa, September 1967, pp. 6–7.

25. Butler and Stokes, pp. 177–80; Rose, *People in Politics*, pp. 126–7; Philip E. Converse, 'Attitudes and Non-Attitudes: Continuation of a Dialogue', in Edward R. Tufte, ed., *The Quantitative Analysis of Social Problems*, Addison–Wesley, Reading, Mass., 1970, pp. 168–89 (mimeo) Survey Research Center, Ann Arbor, February 1964; an earlier version of the Converse paper was read at the Seventeenth International Congress of Psychology in Washington DC, August 1963.

26. David E. RePass, 'Issue Salience and Party Choice', *American Political Science Review*, LXV, June 1971, pp. 389–400.

27. cf. Campbell *et al.*, chapter 5; Butler and Stokes, pp. 36–7, 163–4, 278–92 and 429–31; Peter G. J. Pulzer, *Political Representation and Elections in Britain*, George Allen & Unwin, 1972, pp. 130–31.

28. Commission on the Constitution, pp. 23–7; Sydney Verba and Norman H. Nie, *Participation in America: Political Democracy and Social Equality*, Harper & Row, New York, 1972, pp. 32–40.

29. Almond and Verba, p. 185. However, see *Commission of the*

Constitution, pp. 16–22 and Budge *et al.*, pp. 52–4 and 148–50 for some contradictory data.

30. Verba and Nie, p. 113. Cf. *Commission of the Constitution*, pp. 36–7.

31. James W. Prothro and Charles M. Grigg, 'Fundamental Principles of Democracy; Bases of Agreement and Disagreement', *Journal of Politics*, XXII, 1960, 276–94.

32. Ian Budge, *Agreement and the Stability of Democracy*, Markham, Chicago, 1970, pp. 106–12.

33. ibid., p. 113; cf. Herbert McClosky, 'Consensus and Ideology in American Politics', *American Political Science Review*, LVIII, 1964, 361–82; Samuel Stouffer, *Communism, Conformity and Civil Liberties*, Doubleday, Garden City, NJ, 1955, *passim*.

34. Budge *et al.*, pp. 54–62.

35. Ian Budge and Cornelius O'Leary, 'Cross-Cutting Cleavages, Agreement and Compromise: An Assessment of Three Leading Hypotheses against Scottish and Northern Irish Survey Responses', *Midwest Journal of Political Science*, XV, 1971.

36. cf. Richard Rose, *Governing Without Consensus: An Irish Perspective*, Beacon Press, Boston, 1972, p. 194; Miller and Miller, 'Tables on Political Protest'; Gallup, pp. 1884, 1933, 1971.

37. cf. Erikson and Luttbeg, pp. 45–50 and 56–7.

38. cf. Budge, pp. 106–12; Prothro and Grigg; McClosky.

39. See the discussion of Mill's *Considerations on Representative Government* in chapter 2 above.

40. cf. Butler and Stokes, pp. 200–214; Philip E. Converse, 'The Nature of Belief Systems in Mass Publics', in David E. Apter, ed., *Ideology and Discontent*, The Free Press, New York, pp. 206–61.

41. cf. Lloyd A. Free and Hadley Cantril, *The Political Beliefs of Americans: A Study of Public Opinion*, Rutgers University Press, New Brunswick, New Jersey, 1967, chapter 8 and appendix C.

42. Former Senator J. W. Fulbright and Senator Henry M. Jackson personify this phenomenon. The former is best known for his liberal statesmanship as chairman of the Foreign Relations Committee, but his domestic record accorded very well with that of his Southern colleagues. Jackson, on the other hand, has a hawkish record on defence policy, but he is perhaps best known as a liberal for his domestic policies. Cf. Flanigan, p. 97; Jerrold Rusk and Herbert Weisberg, 'Dimensions of Candidate Evaluation', *American Political Science Review*, LXIV, December 1970,

pp. 1167–85; Arthur H. Miller, Warren E. Miller, Alden S. Raine, and Thad A. Brown, 'A Majority Party in Disarray: Policy Polarization in the 1972 Election', *American Political Science Review*, LXX, September 1976, pp. 753–78. On the lack of consistent ideological position on domestic and foreign issues in Britain, see Butler and Stokes, pp. 195–200.

43. Butler and Stokes, p. 76 report that nearly eight in ten who identify with the middle class call themselves Conservatives while slightly more than seven in ten who identify with the working class call themselves Laborites.

44. cf. Jean Blondel, *Voters, Parties and Leaders: The Social Fabric of British Politics*, Penguin Books, Harmondsworth, 1963, p. 84; Richard Rose, *Politics in England*, Little, Brown & Co., Boston, 1974, pp. 304–5; Richard Shepherd, 'Leadership, Public Opinion, and the Referendum', *Political Quarterly*, XLVI, January to March 1975, pp. 25–35.

45. cf. Rose, *Politics in England*, pp. 304–5; Erikson and Luttbeg, p. 90; Everett Carl Ladd, Jr and Charles D. Hadley, *Political Parties and Political Issues: Patterns in Differentiation Since the New Deal*, Sage Professional Papers in American Politics, Vol. 1, series 04–010, Sage Publications, 1973, p. 35.

46. cf. Rose, *Politics in England*, pp. 160–67; Norman Nie and Kirsti Andersen, 'Mass Belief Systems Revisited: Political Change and Attitude Structure', *Journal of Politics*, XXXVI, August 1974, pp. 540–91; John C. Pierce, 'Party Identification and the Role of Ideology in American Politics', *Midwest Journal of Political Science*, XIV, February 1970, pp. 25–42; Gerald M. Pomper, 'From Confusion to Clarity; Issues and American Voters 1952–68', *American Political Science Review*, LXVI, June 1972, pp. 415–28; Gerald M. Pomper, 'Toward a More Responsible Two-Party System, What Again?' *Journal of Politics*, XXXIII, 1971, pp. 916–40; Almond and Verba, pp. 121–2, 176, 204–9. But for some caveats, see: Michael Margolis, 'From Confusion to Confusion: Issues and the American Voter (1962–72)', *American Political Science Review*, LXXI, March 1977, pp. 31–43.

47. The root words, from which the word Utopia derives, translate from the Greek as 'not a place'. Such a designation is hardly one befitting a theory that purports to describe a system of government that can operate in the real world.

48. On the difference between liberalism and democracy, see chapter 2.

Chapter 5: Revised Theories of Democracy (pp. 95–124)

1. Arthur F. Bentley, *The Process of Government: A Study of Social Pressures*, University of Chicago Press, Chicago, 1908. Citations refer to Peter H. Odegard, ed., Cambridge, Mass., Belknap (Harvard) Press, 1967, which contains a facsimile of the 1908 edition.
2. ibid., p. 201.
3. Odegard, pp. xxx–xxxvi.
4. David Truman, *The Governmental Process*, A. A. Knopf, New York, 1951; Bertram Gross, *The Legislative Struggle*, McGraw-Hill, New York, 1953.
5. Truman, chapter 16; Gross, chapters 1 and 21.
6. cf. Robert A. Dahl, *A Preface to Democratic Theory*, University of Chicago Press, Chicago, 1956; William Kornhauser, *The Politics of Mass Society*, The Free Press, Glencoe, Ill., 1959; Seymour M. Lipset, *Political Man*, Doubleday, New York, 1960.
7. cf. Robert A. Dahl, 'A Critique of the Ruling Elite Model', *American Political Science Review*, LII, 1958, pp. 463–9; Robert A. Dahl, *Who Governs? Democracy and Power in an American City*, Yale University Press, New Haven, 1961; Nelson A. Polsby, *Community Power and Political Theory*, Yale University Press, New Haven, 1963.
8. Samuel Beer, 'Pressure Groups and Parties in Great Britain', *American Political Science Review*, L, 1956, 1–23; Samuel Beer, 'Group Representation in Britain and the United States', *Annals*, CCCXIX, 1958, pp. 130–40; Samuel Finer, *Anonymous Empire: A Study of the Lobby in Great Britain*, Faber & Faber, 1961.
9. Samuel Beer, *British Politics in the Collectivist Age*, Vintage Books, Random House, New York, 1969, pp. 319–20; 321; and 337. See also Hugh Heclo and Aaron Wildavsky, *The Private Government of Public Money*, University of California Press, Berkeley, 1974.
10. Bernard Crick, *In Defence of Politics*, Penguin Books, Harmondsworth, 1962, chapters 3, 7.
11. Graham Wallas, *Human Nature in Politics*, London, 1908. Citations refer to the fourth edition with Foreword by A. L. Rowse, Constable & Company, 1948.
12. Wallas, ibid., pp. 229–30.
13. ibid., p. 240.
14. Martin J. Wiener, *Between Two Worlds: The Political Thought of Graham Wallas*, Clarendon Press, Oxford, 1971, chapter 7.

15. cf. Wallas, pp. 82–92.
16. cf. Beer, pp. 79–102; R. T. McKenzie, *British Political Parties: The Distribution of Power within the Conservative and Labour Parties*, Praeger, New York, 1966, pp. 605–31. The first edition was published by Macmillan in 1954.
17. cf. Pendleton Herring, *The Politics of Democracy: American Parties in Action*, Norton, New York, 1940.
18. E. E. Schattschneider, *Party Government*, Holt, Rinehart & Winston, New York, 1942, chapter 3; E. E. Schattschneider, *The Semi-Sovereign People*, Dryden Press, Hinsdale, Ill., 1960; Committee on Political Parties of the American Political Science Association, *Toward a More Responsible Two-Party System*, Supplement to *American Political Science Review*, XLVIII, 1950; James M. Burns, *Congress on Trial*, Harper & Row, New York, 1949; James M. Burns, *The Deadlock of Democracy: Four Party Politics in America*, Prentice-Hall, Englewood Cliffs, NJ: 1963.
19. Joseph A. Schumpeter, *Capitalism, Socialism and Democracy*, third edition, Harper Torchbooks, New York, 1962, p. 250. This edition contains a facsimile of the original 1942 edition.
20. ibid., p. 269.
21. cf. Dahl, *Preface to Democratic Theory*, pp. 76–7.
22. Paul A. Beck, 'The Role of Agents in Political Socialization', in Stanley Renshon, ed., *Handbook of Political Socialization: Theory and Research*, Free Press, New York, 1976.
23. cf. R. M. Punnett, *British Government and Politics*, second edition, Norton, New York, 1971, pp. 15–17; Richard Rose, *Politics in England*, second edition, Little, Brown & Co., Boston, 1974, pp. 153–67.
24. Edward S. Greenberg, 'Children and Government: A Comparison Across Racial Lines', in Susan Welch and John Comer, eds., *Public Opinion: Its Formation, Measurement and Impact*, Mayfield, Palo Alto, Cal., 1975, pp. 251–76; Edgar Litt, 'Civic Education Norms and Political Indoctrination', *American Sociological Review*, 28, 1963, pp. 69–75.
25. See the discussion in chapter 4, pp. 86–90, above.
26. In their study of the civic culture of five nations, only in Italy did Almond and Verba find any significant objection to inter-party marriages. See Gabriel Almond and Sydney Verba, *The Civic Culture: Political Attitudes and Democracy in Five Nations*, Little, Brown & Co., Boston, 1965, pp. 94–104.
27. cf. Paul A. Beck, 'A Socialization Theory of Partisan Realign-

ment', in Richard Niemi *et al.*, *The Politics of Future Citizens*, Jossey-Bass, San Francisco, 1974; Rose, pp. 172–3; Norman Nie, Sydney Verba and John Petrocik, *The Changing American Voter*, Harvard University Press, Cambridge, Mass., 1976, chapter 5.

28. cf. Ian Budge and Cornelius O'Leary, *Belfast: Approach to Crisis*, Macmillan, London, 1973; Richard Rose, *Governing without Consensus: An Irish Perspective*, Beacon Press, Boston, 1972; James M. Kellas *The Scottish Political System*, Cambridge University Press, Cambridge, 1975; on racial conflict in the United States, see *Supplemental Studies for the National Advisory Commission on Civil Disorders*, US Printing Office, Washington, DC, 1968.

29. cf. Ian Budge *et al.*, *Political Stratification and Democracy*, Macmillan, London, 1972, chapter 4; Rose, *Politics in England*, pp. 228–40; Joseph Trenamen and Denis McQuail, *Television and the Political Image*, Methuen, London, 1961; Jay Blumler and Denis McQuail, *Television in Politics*, Faber & Faber, 1969; Robert Agranoff, ed., *The New Style in Political Campaigns*, second edition, Holbrook, Boston, 1976, *passim*; Edward C. Dreyer and Walter A. Rosenbaum, eds., *Political Opinion and Behavior*, Duxbury, Belmont, Cal., 1976, pp. 153–6 and pp. 175–82. But see also John P. Robinson, 'Perceived Media Bias and the 1968 Vote: Can Media Affect Behavior after all?' in Dreyer and Rosenbaum, eds., pp. 183–91; and Sidney Kraus and Dennis Davis, *The Effects of Mass Communications on Political Behaviour*, Pennsylvania State University Press, 1976, chapter 2.

30. Bernard Berelson, Paul Lazarsfeld, and William McPhee, *Voting*, University of Chicago Press, Chicago, 1954, chapter 14.

31. cf. R. S. Milne and H. C. MacKenzie, *Straight Fight*, Hansard Society, 1954; R. S. Milne and H. C. MacKenzie, *Marginal Seat*, Hansard Society, 1958.

32. Berelson *et al.*, chapter 14.

33. Kornhauser, chapters 1 and 13.

34. Lipset, chapter 4.

35. Peter G. J. Pulzer, *Political Representation and Elections*, George Allen & Unwin, London, 1967, chapter 5.

36. Almond and Verba, chapter 13.

37. Schattschneider, *Semi-Sovereign People*, chapter 8.

38. McKenzie, chapter 11.

39. V. O. Key, *Public Opinion and American Democracy*, A. A. Knopf, New York, 1961, p. 537.

40. Herbert McClosky, 'Consensus and Ideology in American Politics', *American Political Science Review*, LVIII, 1964, pp. 361–82.
41. cf. James M. Burns and Jack Peltason, *Government by the People*, sixth edition, Prentice-Hall, Englewood Cliffs, NJ, 1966; Robert A. Dahl, *Pluralist Democracy in the United States*, Rand McNally, Chicago, 1967; Marian Irish and James Prothro, *The Politics of American Democracy*, fourth edition, Prentice-Hall, Englewood Cliffs, NJ, 1968.
42. Sidney Verba and Norman Nie, *Participation in America: Political Democracy and Social Equality*, Harper & Row, New York, 1972, 40–43.
43. Commission on the Constitution, *Devolution and Other Aspects of Government: An Attitude Survey*, HMSO, 1973, pp. 4–5.
44. *Whitaker's Almanack 1976*, Whitaker, 1975, p. 1117; *Britain 1976: An Official Handbook*, HMSO, 1976, table 38, p. 338; *World Almanac*, 1977, NEA, New York, 1976, pp. 128–43.
45. Verba and Nie, chapters 6 and 18.
46. Mancur Olson, *The Logic of Collective Action: Public Goods and the Theory of Groups*, Harvard University Press, Cambridge, Mass., 1965, pp. 118–41; Robert Salisbury, *Interest Group Politics in America*, Harper & Row, 1970, pp. 32–67.
47. Nie, Verba, and Petrocik, chapter 4; Howard Penniman, ed., *Britain at the Polls: The Parliamentary Elections of 1974*, American Enterprise Institute, Washington DC, 1975, pp. 44–5, 58–60, 68–70 and appendix.
48. Michael Margolis, 'From Confusion to Confusion: Issues and the Electorate 1952–1972', *American Political Science Review*, LXXI, 1977, Table 4.
49. Nie, Verba and Petrocik, pp. 278–81; W. D. Burnham, 'American Politics in the 1970s: Beyond Party?' in William Nisbet Chambers and Walter Dean Burnham, ed., *The American Party System: Stages of Political Development*, second edition, Oxford University Press, New York, 1975, pp. 308–57.
50. Ivor Crewe, 'Do Butler and Stokes Really Explain Change in Britain?' *European Journal of Political Research*, II, 1974, pp. 47–92.
51. Robert Jackman, 'Political Elites, Mass Publics, and Support for Democratic Principles', *Journal of Politics*, XXXIV, 1972, pp. 753–73.
52. cf. Arthur Miller, 'Political Issues and Trust in Government', *American Political Science Review*, LXVIII, 1974, pp. 951–72; also Nie, Verba and Petrocik, chapter 15; Arnold J. Heiden-

heimer, ed., *Political Corruption: Readings in Comparative Analysis*, Holt, Rinehart & Winston, New York, 1970; Carl Bernstein and Bob Woodward, *All the President's Men*, Warner Books, New York, 1976; nor is there reason to be sanguine about the future now that Jimmy-I-will-never-Lie-to-you-Carter has been elected President. In September 1976 Carter sent W. Averell Harriman as a special representative to talk to Leonid I. Brezhnev about the possible effects his election would have on American foreign policy. ' "A lot of time was spent on my explaining to him what an American campaign was all about and what candidates were thinking about," the eighty-four year old diplomat declared ... "It's awfully hard to understand the workings of an American campaign," Mr Harriman observed. "But I think I did some good. I think he was somewhat relieved by what I had to say. I'm sure he wasn't totally satisfied. *I'm not sure I was able to persuade him that everything that was said was of no importance.*" ' *New York Times*, 21 September 1976, p. 1 (italics added).

53. Lipset, Part I; Kornhauser, Part 3 and conclusion; Dorothy Pickles, *Democracy*, Penguin Books Inc., Baltimore, MD, 1972, chapter 10.

54. cf. Charles McCoy and John Playford, eds., *Apolitical Politics: A Critique of Behavioralism*, Thomas Crowell, New York, 1967; Henry S. Kariel, ed., *Frontiers of Democratic Theory*, Random House, New York, 1970; Peter Bachrach, *The Theory of Democratic Elitism*, Little, Brown & Co., Boston, 1967; William Connolly, ed., *The Bias of Pluralism*, Atherton, New York, 1969; William A. Gamson, 'Stable Unrepresentation in American Society', *American Behavioral Scientist*, XII, 1968, pp. 15–21; John Plamenatz, *Democracy and Illusion: An Examination of Certain Aspects of Modern Democratic Theory*, Longman, 1973.

55. Herbert Storing, ed., *Essays on the Scientific Study of Politics*, Holt, Rinehart & Winston, New York, 1962; Bernard Crick, *The American Science of Politics*, Routledge & Kegan Paul, 1959.

56. Bert A. Rockman, 'A "Behavioral" Evaluation of the Critique of Behavioralism', a paper delivered at the annual meeting of the American Political Association, New York, September 1969; Robert A. Dahl, *After the Revolution*, Yale University Press, New Haven, 1970, Part 3.

57. Michael Margolis, 'The New American Government Textbooks', *American Journal of Political Science*, XVII, 1973, 457–63.

58. cf. J. P. Mackintosh, *The Government and Politics of Britain*, Hutchinson, London, 1970; A. H. Hanson and Malcolm Walles, *Governing Britain*, Fontana/Collins, 1970, chapter 8; Trevor Smith, *Anti-Politics: Consensus, Reform and Protest in Britain*, Charles Knight, London, 1972.

Chapter 6: The Death of Democracy (pp. 125–55)

1. John Stuart Mill, *Considerations of Representative Government*, chapter 3.
2. UPI dispatch, Harrisburg, PA, 4 April 1973.
3. *Appropriation Accounts (Volume 3: Classes X-XV and XVIII): 1974–75*, HMSO, 1976, pp. 156–7.
4. cf. William J. Keefe and Morris S. Ogul, *The American Legislative Process*, fourth edition, Prentice-Hall, Englewood Cliffs, NJ, 1977, pp. 26–7; Richard Rose, *Politics in England*, second edition, Little, Brown & Co., Boston, 1974, p. 247.
5. Rose, p. 90.
6. cf. Robert Presthus, *Public Administration*, sixth edition, The Ronald Press, New York, 1975, p. 39.
7. Approximately 90 per cent of contract funds for weapons development are allocated on a non-competitive basis. See William Proxmire, 'The Pentagon Versus Free Enterprise', *Saturday Review*, January 1970.
8. See *Statistical Abstract of the United States: 1976*, Bureau of the Census, Washington DC, 1976, pp. 292–3; also George F. Will, 'The Hot Seat,' *Newsweek*, 7 March 1977, p. 96.
9. Raymond Vernon, *Sovereignty at Bay*, Basic Books, New York, 1971, p. 5.
10. Two notable exceptions are C. Wright Mills, *The Power Elite*, Oxford University Press, New York, 1956, which dealt with the emerging dominance of the executive, military and corporations over the legislatures, and Herbert Marcuse, *One Dimensional Man*, Beacon Press, Boston, 1964, which denoted how modern capitalist institutions succeed in creating what Marx would have called a 'false consciousness' among ordinary citizens.
11. Vernon, p. 32; also *Directory of Corporate Affiliations, 1976*, National Register Publishing Company, Skokie, Ill., 1976, p. 177.
12. cf. Richard Barnett and Ronald Müller, *Global Reach*, Simon & Shuster, New York, 1974, pp. 266–7.
13. cf. John K. Galbraith, *The New Industrial State*, New American Library, Signet, New York, 1967, *passim* and John K. Galbraith,

Economics and the Public Purpose, New American Library, Signet, New York, 1975, Part 3.

14. S. David Freeman, *Energy and the New Era*, Vintage Books, New York, 1974, pp. 152–5.

15. *International Herald Tribune*, New York Times–Washington Post, Paris, 24 April 1974. Report of hearings of Senate Permanent Subcommittee on Investigations. Of course the companies did not truckle totally to the demands of the Arab states. To avoid closing down their Dutch refineries when the Arabs banned all Mideast Crude from Holland, (Holland was considered overly friendly with Israel) the oil companies shuffled tankers and managed miraculously to land only 'Nigerian' crude at Rotterdam.

16. When the General Accounting Office of the Congress wanted to see company cash flow records for certain commercial projects before recommending approval of a $250m. loan to Lockheed Corporation in 1970, the Defense Department and Lockheed refused to produce the information on grounds of confidentiality. See *Congressional Quarterly Weekly Report*, 9 February 1971, pp. 431–3.

17. cf. Barnett and Müller, Chapter 10; *Report of the Census of Production*, HMSO, 1968.

18. Barnett and Müller, pp. 16ff; *Britain 1974, An Official Handbook*, HMSO, 1974, p. 238.

19. *Britain 1974*, p. 219.

20. Edward S. Greenberg, *Serving the Few: Corporate Capitalism and the Bias of Government Policy*, John Wiley & Co., New York, 1974, p. 46.

21. Richard Whitely, 'The City and Industry: the directors of large companies, their characteristics and connections', in Philip Stanworth and Anthony Giddens, eds., *Elites and Power in British Society*, Cambridge University Press, 1974, chapter 4.

22. General Motors Chevrolet Division produced a bicentennial ditty that epitomized the corporation's attempt to appropriate the symbols of popular culture for its products. American television viewers heard:

Baseball, hot dogs, apple pie, and Chevrolet
They go together in the good old USA.

Unbeknownst to most Americans, apropos of no special celebration, South Africans heard over their newly instituted television network:

Braaivleis (Barbeques), rugby, sunny skies and Chevrolet,
They go together in the good old RSA.

So much for Chevrolet's special identification with America.

23. Stefan Robock and Kenneth Simmonds, *International Business and Multinational Enterprises*, Irwin-Dorsey, Homewood, Ill., 1973, pp. 37–8.

24. cf. *Statistical Abstract 1976*, Tables 648, 693, and 694; Joseph Pechman and Benjamin Okner, *Who Bears the Tax Burden?* Brookings, Washington, DC, 1974, *passim*; John Urry and John Wakeford, eds., *Power in Britain: Sociological Readings*, Heinemann, 1976, chapters 2 and 4; Central Statistical Service, *Social Trends*, 7 November 1976, HMSO, 1976, tables 5.4 and 5.36.

25. cf. *New York Times*, 24 August 1975, Section F; Ralph Nader and Mark Green, 'Crime in the Suites', *New Republic*, 166, 29 April 1972, pp. 17–21.

26. cf. Christopher J. Hewitt, 'Elites and the Distribution of Power in British Society', in Giddens and Stanworth, chapter 3; Robert Dahl, *Who Governs?* Yale University Press, New Haven, 1961, chapter 28.

27. See the discussion of pluralism in chapter 5.

28. Maurice Duverger, *Modern Democracies: Economic Power Versus Political Power*, The Dryden Press, Hinsdale, Ill., 1974, p. 191.

29. Ironically it is the richer liberal-democratic nations which are succeeding with programmes of voluntary birth control. These nations may have to bring severe pressure on the citizens of poorer nations to force them to curtail population growth, for their own good. That is, liberal democrats may end up compelling these less fortunate citizens 'to be free'.

30. cf. Elizabeth and David Dodson Gray; William F. Martin, *Growth and Its Implications for the Future*, The Dinosaur Press, Branford, Conn., 1975, chapter 2; Amory B. Lovins, *World Energy Strategies: Facts, Issues and Options*, Earth Resources Research Ltd, 1973, *passim*.

31. cf. Robert Heilbroner, *An Inquiry into the Human Propect*, W. W. Norton, New York, 1975, chapters 3–4.

32. cf. E. F. Schumacher, *Small is Beautiful: Economics as if People Mattered*, Perennial Press, Harper & Row, New York, 1975, Part III, chapter 1; Ronald H. Chilcote and Joel C. Edelstein, 'Alternative Perspectives of Development and Underdevelopment in Latin America', in Chilcote and Edelstein, eds., *Latin America: The Struggle with Dependency and Beyond*, Schenkman, Mass., 1974, pp. 1–87.

33. cf. Schumacher, Part IV; Edward Goldsmith *et al.*, *Blueprint*

for *Survival*, New American Library, New York, 1974; Mancur Olson and Hans H. Landsberg, eds., *The No-Growth Society*, W. W. Norton, New York, 1974 (reprint of *Daedalus*, Autumn 1973).

Chapter 7: Viable Democracy (pp. 156–87)

1. See chapter 1 for a discussion of the terms 'participation' and 'politics'.
2. See chapter 4, section 4, 'The Average Citizen in Fact', for a discussion of citizens' knowledge of political issues.
3. cf. Ian Budge *et al.*, *Political Stratification and Democracy*, Macmillan, 1972, chapter 4; Edward C. Dreyer and Walter A. Rosenbaum, *Political Opinion and Behavior*, third edition, Duxbury Press, North Scituate, Mass., 1976, pp. 152–8.
4. cf. J. W. Fulbright, *The Pentagon Propaganda Machine*, Vintage Books, New York, 1971, chapter 2; Richard Rose, *Politics in England*, second edition, Little, Brown & Co., Boston, 1974, chapter 7.
5. Geoffrey Wolff, 'Government Book Control', *New York Herald Tribune and Washington Post*, Paris edition, 9 February 1967.
6. cf. Ithiel de Sola Pool, ed., *Talking Back: Citizen Feedback and Cable Technology*, MIT Press, Cambridge, Mass., 1973, chapters 1 and 5.
7. cf. John Kemeny, *Man and the Computer*, Charles Scribners, New York, 1972, chapter 2.
8. See Robert Paul Wolff, *In Defense of Anarchism*, Harper Torchbooks, New York, 1970, pp. 34–7, for a proposal for 'instant direct democracy'.
9. On technical and administrative controls of computerized files, see Stanley Rothman and Charles Mosmann, *Computers and Society*, second edition, Scientific Research Associates, Chicago, 1976, chapter 18.
10. cf. David J. Farber, 'Networks: An Introduction', *Datamation*, April 1972, pp. 36–9.
11. cf. Rothman and Mosmann, chapter 15; Privacy Protection Study Commission, *Personal Privacy in an Information Society*, US Government Printing Office, Washington DC, July 1977, *passim*.
12. See chapter 2, section 1, 'Liberalism and Democracy'.
13. cf. Gilbert Gillespie, *Public Access Cable Television in the United States and Canada*, Praeger, New York, 1975, chapter 1; Pool, chapter 5; but for some caveats about the likelihood of the

spread of cable television in the United States, see Anne W. Branscomb, 'The Cable Fable: Will it Come True?' *Journal of Communication,* XXV, Winter 1975, 44–56.

14. *Report of the Committee on the Future of Broadcasting,* Cmnd 6753, HMSO 1977 (the report is summarized and discussed in several articles in *The Times,* 25 March 1977). See also 'Over to Milton Keynes', *Economist,* 24 January 1976, p. 24.

15. Other technologies, such as telephone are usable for networks, but there are still capitalization problems of providing enough lines and of upgrading the information transmission rates of existing lines. See Kemeny, chapter 10, and Rothman and Mosman, chapter 4.

16. cf. Louis Harris and Associates, *Confidence and Concern: Citizens View American Government,* Regal Books/Kings Court Communications, Cleveland, Ohio, 1974, pp. 9–11; Gabriel Almond and Sydney Verba, *The Civic Culture; Political Attitudes and Democracy in Five Nations,* Little, Brown & Co., Boston, 1965, chapter 5.

17. See chapter 3 for a discussion of Rousseau and other critics of liberal democracy.

18. Robert A. Dahl, *After the Revolution?: Authority in a Good Society,* Yale University Press, New Haven, Conn., 1970, chapter 2; John K. Galbraith, *Economics and the Public Purpose,* Signet, New York, 1973, Part 3; Amory Lovins, 'Resilience in Energy Strategy', *New York Times,* 24 July 1977, p. E17; Morton Mintz and Jerry S. Cohen, *American, Inc.; Who Owns and Operates the United States,* Dial Press, New York, 1971, prologue and chapter 1; E. F. Schumacher, *Small is Beautiful: Economics as if People Mattered,* Perennial Press, Harper & Row, New York, 1975, *passim.*

19. cf. Lovins; Galbraith, chapters 10–11; Mintz and Cohen, pp. 41–4.

20. cf. Dahl, pp. 59–63; In 1969 Norman Mailer and Jimmy Breslin campaigned for the mayoralty of New York with the promise of seeking statehood for the city.

21. MPs have no personal staff. They receive a small grant for secretarial service, but it is inadequate to pay for employing one person full-time. Regional, state, and local government officials in both Britain and the United States generally do not have personal staff either. Staff usually are assigned to the committees of the council or legislature, and they often are available only at the behest of committee officers.

22. The existence of a common interest, public interest, or general will is a basic assumption of liberal democracy. See chapter 2, section 1 above. For some additional discussion of this concept, see Brian Barry, 'The Public Interest', in William Connolly, ed., *The Bias of Pluralism*, Atherton, New York, 1969, pp. 159–77 and Glendon Schubert, 'The Public Interest in Administrative Decision-Making', *American Political Science Review*, LI, June 1957, pp. 346–68.

23. cf. Edward Weisband and Thomas Franck, *Resignation in Protest*, Penguin Books, Harmondsworth, 1975, chapters 3 and 7.

24. cf. John K. Galbraith, *The New Industrial State*, Signet Books, New York, 1967, chapter 6.

25. Dahl, pp. 130–31; also Adolf Sturmthal, 'Workers' Councils' in Terrance Cook and Patrick Morgan, eds., *Participatory Democracy*, Canfield Press, San Francisco, 1971, pp. 358–70.

26. cf. Schumacher, Part IV, chapter 2.

27. ibid., Part IV, chapter 5.

28. cf. Cook and Morgan, chapter 1.

29. cf. Bernard Crick, *The Reform of Parliament*, Weidenfeld & Nicolson, 1968, chapter 10; William J. Keefe and Morris S. Ogul, *The American Legislative Process: Congress and the States*, fourth edition, Prentice Hall, Englewood Cliffs, NJ, 1977, chapter 14.

30. cf. Peter Woll, *American Bureaucracy*, second edition, Norton, New York, 1977, chapter 6; Trevor Smith, *Anti-Politics – Consensus, Reform and Protest in Britain*, Charles Knight, 1972, chapter 2.

31. cf. Wolff; B. F. Skinner, *Walden Two*, Macmillan, New York, 1948; editions of *Walden Two* were still in print in 1976 in both the United States and the United Kingdom.

32. See chapter 3, section 4.

33. Schumacher, pp. 259–60.

34. Herbert Marcuse, 'New Forms of Control', in Albert H. Teich, ed., *Technology and Man's Future*, St Martin's Press, New York, 1972, p. 76; (the article is chapter 1 of *One-Dimensional Man*).

35. On the rationality of citizen activity, see chapter 5, section 5, (especially pp. 116–20 ff.).

Index